OM 285
2/2

A Coach's Guide to Asset Mapping Teacher Quality:
The Journey from Compliance to Community

A Coach's Guide to Asset Mapping Teacher Quality:
The Journey from Compliance to Community

Foundation Building-Year One

Lorraine Richardson
Owl Mountain Coaching, Inc.
Detroit, Michigan

A Coach's Guide to Asset Mapping Teacher Quality:
The Journey from Compliance to Community

Lorraine Richardson© 2011
All Rights Reserved
Originally published and copyrighted under the title:
The Journey from Compliance to Community© 2006

You may edit, modify, integrate your experience, expertise, and wisdom into the "conversations" presentation materials, or worksheets in the guide/workbook to fit your professional needs.

There are a few restrictions:

- You may **not modify** and/or sell the Owl Mountain Coaching Asset-Mapping System© in *any* language.
- You may **not** use the Owl Mountain Coaching™ or Conversations with a Coach™ logos to market or sell your work without written permission.
- You may use the Owl Mountain Coaching Asset Mapping principles and activities to create a virtual community of practice with or for others as long as they are not charged a fee to participate.
- You may reproduce the activities in the workbook for the purpose of training classroom teachers.
- Whatever derivatives you create should provide attribution to Owl Mountain Coaching, Inc. Lorraine Richardson.

Warning and disclaimer:
Every effort has been made to make this guide as complete and as accurate as possible, but no warranty or fitness is implied. The information supplied is on an "as is" basis. The author or publisher shall have neither liability nor responsibility to any person or entity with respect to any loss or damages arising directly or indirectly from any information contained in this book.

1. Instructional Coach 2. Literacy Coach 3. Teacher Attrition 4. New Teachers 5. Urban Teachers 6. Professional Learning Communities 7. Lead Teachers 8. Retired Educators 9. Asset Mapping 10. Teacher Quality 11. Classroom Practices 12. Parent Leaders 13. Teacher Leaders 14. Supervising Teachers 15 Turnaround Coaching 16. Systemic Change 17. Reform Model 18. Classroom Management

ISBN   978-0-55767095-6

Table of Contents

Dedication

This work is dedicated to the retired educators who labor to pass the torch to the next generation of teachers in underserved communities. As they share their experience, expertise, and wisdom about teacher quality and classroom practices, they become members of an intergenerational movement working to strengthen the educational capital of America.

Acknowledgments

I would like to express my gratitude to the many educators with whom I have worked with over the years to produce the ideas that are presented in this guide. To the hundreds of teachers and the thousands of students in whose classrooms I have labored, you have been my greatest motivation and inspiration.

My special thanks to Dr. Sarah Gibson, former principal, an Oakland University professor who is still passing the torch, and a premier educator who started me on my professional "journey" of growth and change. The "journey" began when an eighth grader made tracks to Dr. Gibson's office to complain about a failing grade on her book report. The student had copied it from a sibling I had taught the previous year. Dr. Gibson's pattern for handling discipline problems was to sit with students to determine what they were learning in class. When Dr. Gibson informed me that the student really didn't understand the assignment and that was why she had cheated, I informed her that I "told" the class what I expected. Her even-toned, non-emotional reply was, "If telling were teaching, everyone would be smart."

Wanting to convince my boss that I really was doing my job, I remained after school one afternoon in 1978 to rearrange the desks and to revise my seating plan in order that the half of the class that understood what I "told" them could interface with the half that did not. Before the research of Johnson and Johnson or Spencer Kagan, I started on my "journey," with Dr. Gibson's support, toward turning my classroom into a collaborative, rich, and rigorous learning community with a heart.

Preface

Throughout my career as an urban teacher, literacy coach, instructional coach, workshop designer and presenter, I have gained tremendous insight into the anatomy of successful urban classrooms.

Working in the classrooms hundreds of teachers to help them improve their performance, and providing professional development over a period of fifteen years, I have found that highly effective teachers exhibit similar abilities, beliefs, skills, and strengths (assets) . Analyzing and disaggregating these attributes, I developed activities, ideas, materials, tools, and workshops to support those teachers who are less effective.

Being a teacher of teachers meant that I was a quasi-administrator, but not a promoted administrator. In order to gain entry into the classrooms of my peers, I had to create non-threatening, non-judgmental protocols. So, at the beginning of each school year, I designed a special "make me or break me" workshop to provide some of the credibility needed to break the ice and to begin to gain entry. Later, visiting teachers individually for a friendly chat and follow-up, I provided each with a form outlining services I could provide (See Appendix A).

As I continued to support schools and teachers in my retirement, I became concerned about the many classrooms still built on a model of compliance. I hail from the one-industry state that put the world on wheels. More than the other forty-nine, we prepared our students for a manufacturing economy. Too many of our schools, especially high schools, taught and reinforced a covert curriculum of passive obedience, rigid uniformity, punctuality, silence, and rote learning through memorization (Alvin Toffler, *Future Shock).*

So, I began to think about how to move more teachers (and their students) from working in compliant classrooms to working in classrooms based on community, where the social, emotional, and cognitive aspects of learning are blended.

However, often teachers are expected to change their teaching behavior without the "conversations" and the reflections that support altering their thinking patterns (Costa and Garmston, *Cognitive Coaching*). I started creating my asset-mapping system and workbook for the coaches, retired educators, teacher leaders, and other trusted professionals who support teachers. I wanted to share my thoughts, ideas and to provide a conceptual framework for them to engage in collegial and reflective "conversations" with teachers, recreating the coaching mindset that served me so well during my career. Thus, my two companies, Conversations with a Coach™ and Owl Mountain Coaching™, were born, and I set about creating a mission and philosophy statement.

Introduction

Effective coaches persist amid an uncomfortable or inconvenient environment, possess a wealth of problem-solving abilities, and have an iron will.

Coaching Mission and Philosophy

™

As coaches, we are committed to stemming the tide of new and urban teacher attrition that is detrimental to student achievement. Using a job-embedded, ongoing, formative assessment model, we seek to create the teachers and classrooms crucial to teaching problem-solving and cognitive flexibility to ALL of our children.

We are dedicated to providing ongoing opportunities to engage in reflective and collegial conversations about the teaching quality and classroom practices in a non-threatening, supportive manner. We believe that mutually respectful "conversations" can unite teachers and coaches, providing the psychological connections necessary for personal growth, a positive teaching experience, and career longevity. As experienced and trusted professionals, we are committed to an equal regard and to an equal voice.

Committed to an Equal Voice and to an Equal Regard!

Coaching Roles and Responsibilities

Coaching- A process of moving teachers from where they are to where they want or need to be.

Assisting,

Modeling   Facilitating,

Problem solving   Supporting, Helping,

Collaborating,   Listening   Prompting,

Motivating,   Communicating   **Guiding**

Probing   **Challenging**

Encouraging   **Confirming**

Suggesting   **Explaining**

Is this the "Journey"?

Dear Coach,

Although *A Coach's Guide to Asset Mapping Teacher Quality: The Journey from Compliance to Community* is dedicated to retired educators in order that we pass the torch to the next generation of teachers, it can be used by any educator who labors to improve teacher quality and classroom practices.

Whether you are working in a new school where you are building from scratch, or building on an existing educational environment that has or has not made adequate yearly progress (AYP), the Owl Mountain Asset-Mapping™ approach provides a framework for reflecting on your own practice and supplies a foundation for collegial and reflective Conversations with a Coach.

A common challenge for school-district based professional development or university teaching support programs created to assist teachers is the lack of a coherent, conceptual framework and codified system for documenting teacher quality and classroom practices. Owl Mountain Coaching, LLC is open to the challenge. A Coach's Guide to Asset-Mapping Teacher Quality: The Journey from Compliance to Community is codified system that allows for all coaches and teachers to be on the same page.

The "journey" begins at a place called "compliance" and ends at a destination named "community." During three "Stops" on the journey, eighteen principles in three core areas critical to teacher quality are examined, how highly effective teachers:

        Stop 1.0   Establish credibility,
        Stop 2.0   Demonstrate caring,
        Stop 3.0   Create systems (rituals and routines).

The "journey" is a collaborative and participatory process that places ownership of issues and challenges in the hands of teachers enabling you to secure commitment from them to move toward agreed-upon goals. By facilitating the process of inquiry, the coach doesn't own the solution; she helps identify areas of strength and areas for growth.

A Coach's Guide to Asset-Mapping Teacher Quality will support your efforts to make available the "conversations" and expertise new and urban educators need for creating structures that can positively alter the culture of the classroom. Many professions employ coaches who serve as the trusted guide, the catalyst for helping the professional to move past their current level of performance. Probing, confirming, challenging, and explaining, the coach focuses on strengthening the "inner or mental game".

Helping to build the bridge between where teachers are now and where they need to be to meet the needs of today's students, my system moves away from past models of professional development because it is needs-based, ongoing, and job-embedded instead of a one-shot or off-site approach.

How to Use the Guide

Throughout the asset-mapping workbook, the terms "coach," "teacher leader," and "trusted professional" are used interchangeably. The Conversations with a Coach logo represents an opportunity for you to engage in mutually respectful, reflective and sometimes critical "conversations" with teachers.

Context: Where ever you see a blank logo is an opportunity for you to edit or modify what I have written to suit the context of your situation, to integrate your experience, expertise, insights, views and wisdom into my starter "conversations" or information. You may choose to work alone or to establish an online virtual professional learning community (VPLC) using social networks. Through blogging, tweeting, chatting, forums, discussion boards, video chats, you can create a collective intelligence about teacher quality and classroom practices. Decide who you want or need to be on your support team.

The Owl Mountain Coaching Owl symbol represents coaching challenges and wisdom from a "chief owl" perspective. Scattered throughout the guide are five challenges that you might want to use as journaling topics. Think of these tools as personal tests designed to stimulate, strain, and to stretch you while providing you with opportunities to analyze your own practice and to discover who you are as a coach. Journaling requires that you invest in yourself as a coach. Most journals are personal, private records; however, you may choose to share your thoughts with a TRUSTED colleague.

Activities: Included in each core area (how highly effective teachers 1.0 establish credibility, 2.0 demonstrate caring, and 3.0 create systems) are activities that reinforce the eighteen principles effective teachers practice intuitively at an unconscious level. The activities can be used to support teachers with undeveloped or underdeveloped assets and will keep you from having to make up everything as you go.

Review the table of contents, the three core areas, the eighteen principles, and the appendices before getting started.

As a professional development provider, you will be expected to lead workshops and small group meetings. Think about norms you want to put in place, how you want to arrange the room, and how much space is needed for these activities. Remember the mission and philosophy statement of "an equal voice and an equal regard" when planning the seating. Community is created when participants can make eye contact with one another (Peter Block *Community: The Structure of Belonging*).

The companion site for *A Coach's Guide to Asset-Mapping Teacher Quality is*: http://www.owlmountaincoaching.com. If you spot any omissions or have any suggestions, please let me know. The guide is a work-in-progress.

Who Will Coach the Coaches?

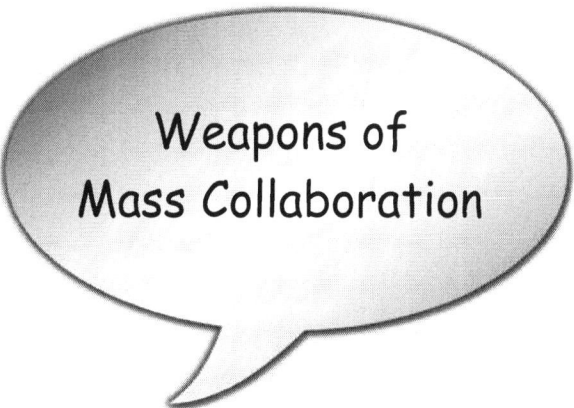

Blogs, Tweets, Chats, Wikis, Forums, Videos, Live Streaming,

Social networking enables online conversations around a community of like-minded individuals. Social networking websites are regularly used by millions of people around the world. Educators, schools, and districts have joined the fray. Social networks are about peering, sharing, socializing, and creating. You can create an individual network (community) around a single educational topic or theme: teacher attrition, the writing process, collaborative learning, classroom management, teacher quality, establishing credibility, school turnaround, etc. (Ascot and Williams, *Wikinomics: How Mass Collaboration Changes Everything*).

Social Networks:
A Global Brain
Peer Support
Co-creation

A social networking, virtual professional learning community (VPLC) will provide you with a platform to vent and connect with others in your situation. Creating a social network allows us to harnesses the skill, intelligence, ingenuity and wisdom of a larger educational community more efficiently than traditional methods of professional development. Nobody is as smart as everybody (*Mavericks at Work: Why the Smartest Minds in Business Win*), thus, individual knowledge turns into the property of the group. The more smart people collectively working on the challenges of teaching and classroom practices, the more likely they are to be solved. In *Think and Grow Rich*, Napolean Hill wrote, *"No two minds ever come together without thereby creating a third, invisible, intangible force which may be likened to a third mind."*

Providing a base of identity, purpose, and pride, a virtual professional learning community will support you on your "journey" to shaping and reshaping what is possible for teacher quality and classroom practices.

Social Networks

Possible groups to be formed may include:

- Public school coaches joining forces with others within the same geographic location
- Charter school teacher leaders collaborating with peers under the same charter management company.
- Content area coaches forming a network with a cluster of schools.
- Grade-level coaches creating a collective network with a cluster of other schools.
- School and university partnerships.

How large do you need the team to be? I belong to www.ning.com community networks with fewer than 100 members, but constantly growing, and others with thousands of members. The idea is to collaborate with colleagues outside of the environment where you work, allowing you to reflect on and share the capacity, skill, and ingenuity of peers, providing a multiplier effect (Tapscott and Williams, *Wikinomics: How Mass Collaboration Changes Everything*). Social networking peers can become critical friends.

Who do you want or need to be on your team (mastermind dream team)? Why?

Challenge: At the end of your "journey", you can/will create the go-to resource guide for starting and sustaining a virtual collaborative coaching community around teacher quality and classroom practices with the ultimate goal of reducing teacher attrition.

Who/ Name	Role/Title/Organization
1.	
2.	
3.	
4.	
5.	
6.	
7.	
8.	
9.	
10.	

Follow me on www.twitter.com/lyrichardson

Towards a Stable Teaching Pipeline:
The Attrition Challenge

Nearly 50 percent of new teachers in America leave the profession during the first five years. In high poverty, high priority communities 50 percent leave during the first three years. Research demonstrates that students assigned to effective teachers for three consecutive years in a row score 49 percent higher on standardized tests than children assigned to less effective teachers three years in a row (National Partnership of Teaching in At-Risk Schools).

Repeated teacher turnover disrupts the stability, continuity, and cohesiveness of a school and thus impedes student achievement. Institutional memory for the content pedagogy, testing programs, and extracurricular activities is an illusion and negatively affects student learning. According to the Alliance for Excellent Education, $2.2 billion is spent annually on new teacher attrition. That amount does not include the money spent on teachers who transfer to other schools or districts seeking better working conditions. Certainly, the taxpayer dollar could be better spent.

How do we address the "turnaround challenge" if every time we turnaround, a school is rebuilding its staff? How do we leave no child behind without a stable teaching pipeline in *every* community across the country?   .

Mission: As coaches, we are committed to stemming the tide of new and urban teacher attrition.

1.   What is the three/five year teacher attrition rate for the school(s) you serve? Identify **five** reasons teachers in your school or district leave the profession.

2.   How much does it cost to replace each teacher who quits the profession in your school district? What does teacher attrition cost your school district/state annually?

3.   What is the teacher attendance/absentee rate for the school? For the district? What are the major reasons teachers are *really* absent?

4.   How many teachers will you coach and why?

Pilot/Inquiry-Based Challenge

Frame Your Coaching Challenge:
Describe the biggest challenge you will face working
to improve teacher quality and ,thus, reduce teacher attrition

Beginning Coaching Goals:

Employing a non-threatening approach, you will work to:

- ✓ Build a shared system of responsibility.
- ✓ Identify areas of strength for teachers to share with others.
- ✓ Practice the reflections that allow change to occur.
- ✓ Identify areas for growth to enhance teachers' career longevity.
- ✓ Assist teachers to move past their current level of performance.
- ✓ Develop and implement promising practices that are grounded in research and theory.
- ✓ Identify challenges that might interfere with a positive teaching experience.
- ✓ Increase teacher efficacy (the belief that one's actions can make a difference).
- ✓ Assist teachers with valuing both process and content.
- ✓ Assist teachers as they reflect on and articulate reasons for their actions.
- ✓ Identify potential conflicts and ethical dilemmas

Additional Goals:

Coaching Reminders for the "journey"

As you begin to create a plan of action, consider the support YOU will need as you start your "journey." You may have process issues, strategies, ideas, readings, research, and next steps that you want to discuss with a peer. Who is on your internal and external team?

As you begin your journey of growth and change, think about the following:

- Starting date/cycle, Closing date/cycle, Frequency of visits.
- What kind of kick-off /initial meeting will you hold? (See the Welcome New Recruits activity or the Examining Teacher Assets: Fired or Rehired writing assignment in Appendix B).
- How will you establish YOUR credibility with teachers and the school? (See Appendix A)
- How will you/can you provide a non-threatening, non-judgmental rapport where change and learning can occur?
- What kind of resistance do you anticipate receiving from teachers or administrators?
- How will you validate teachers and learn their stories? (See Appendix A)
- Where and how do you begin? Which staff members can serve as role models or as a support team?
- How will you share and document the results of your work with teachers? Where will the results reside?
- How do you want to write up and share the collaborative efforts of your coaching community?

Best wishes to you on your "journey" of change.

Lorraine Richardson, Chief Owl

Strengthening America, One Conversation and
One Classroom at a Time.

Owl Mountain Coaching Personal Challenge One

Journal Entry: Why Me? Why Now?

"Writing holds us responsible for our words and ultimately makes us more thoughtful human beings." Ernest Boyer

- ✓ How do you define the term "coach"?
- ✓ What gives you the *moral authority* or the right to be a coach, to work directly with classroom teachers?
- ✓ What are **your** "assets"?
- ✓ What would you like for others to say about you at the end of the year or coaching cycle?
- ✓ Write a vision statement for your role as a coach. What do you hope to accomplish?

*Have you identified a **trusted peer** to share the insights from your journal?*

Notes

"We don't receive wisdom; we must discover it for ourselves after a journey that no one can take for us or spare us." Marcel Proust

The Journey from Compliance to Community

Mastering the craft of coaching/teaching is an ongoing process of reflection and revision. Becoming a coach/teacher is like embarking on a "journey".

Classroom Transformation:
The Journey from Compliance to Community

Students come to us at risk and the environment we create, or fail to create, further puts them at risk. On this "journey," teachers working with a coach, teacher leader, retired educator, or other trusted professional will begin to examine their role as they paint the environment on which learning is built, a place that replaces homes and communities lost.

It is a supportive environment that allows students to grow intellectually and emotionally. The success of the school year for both the students and the teacher depends on this dynamic.

Too many classrooms today are built on compliance, classrooms designed to prepare students for a manufacturing-based society. In a compliant classroom, the teacher makes all the rules and decisions. A premium is placed on "physical quietude, on silence and rigid uniformity" (John Dewey). Compliance is a classroom culture of students working daily at unmonitored seatwork or at a computer screen as teachers repeatedly sit at their desks. It is a culture of students and teachers entering into a bargain of easy grades for good behavior; it is a peace-at-any-price environment. Limited support is offered for listening, speaking, reading to, and writing for an authentic audience. Students are often expected to master concepts and ideas that they have never processed through discussion (oral rehearsal, a brain-friendly activity).

In a community, learning is both a social and a cognitive act. Students and teachers collaborate; they form a bond, become a family unit, and belong. Community promotes an environment in which troublesome behavior is solved together. Community encourages students to reflect on how they can live and learn together. Seating becomes social and cognitive engineering. In addition to learning the content, students engage in learning lessons about trust, fair play, forgiveness, sharing, and respect—values they may not experience at home.

In a community, seating becomes social engineering.

A community supports authentic learning and self-assessment. Classroom 2.0 is a seminar that empowers students to become proactive agents of their own learning process, in an environment that nurtures hidden talents, promotes traits (risk-taking, maverick thinking, marching to a different drummer) necessary for success in a twenty-first century, innovation-based global economy. We are in uncharted territory.

In moving from compliance to community, compromise must take place between a system that requires narrow obedience with a system that promotes autonomy in the social and intellectual realms (Alfie Kohn). On The Journey from Compliance to Community, the teacher develops an emotionally safe, orderly, and democratic community that promotes interpersonal sensibilities and intellectual health.

The Journey from Compliance to Community

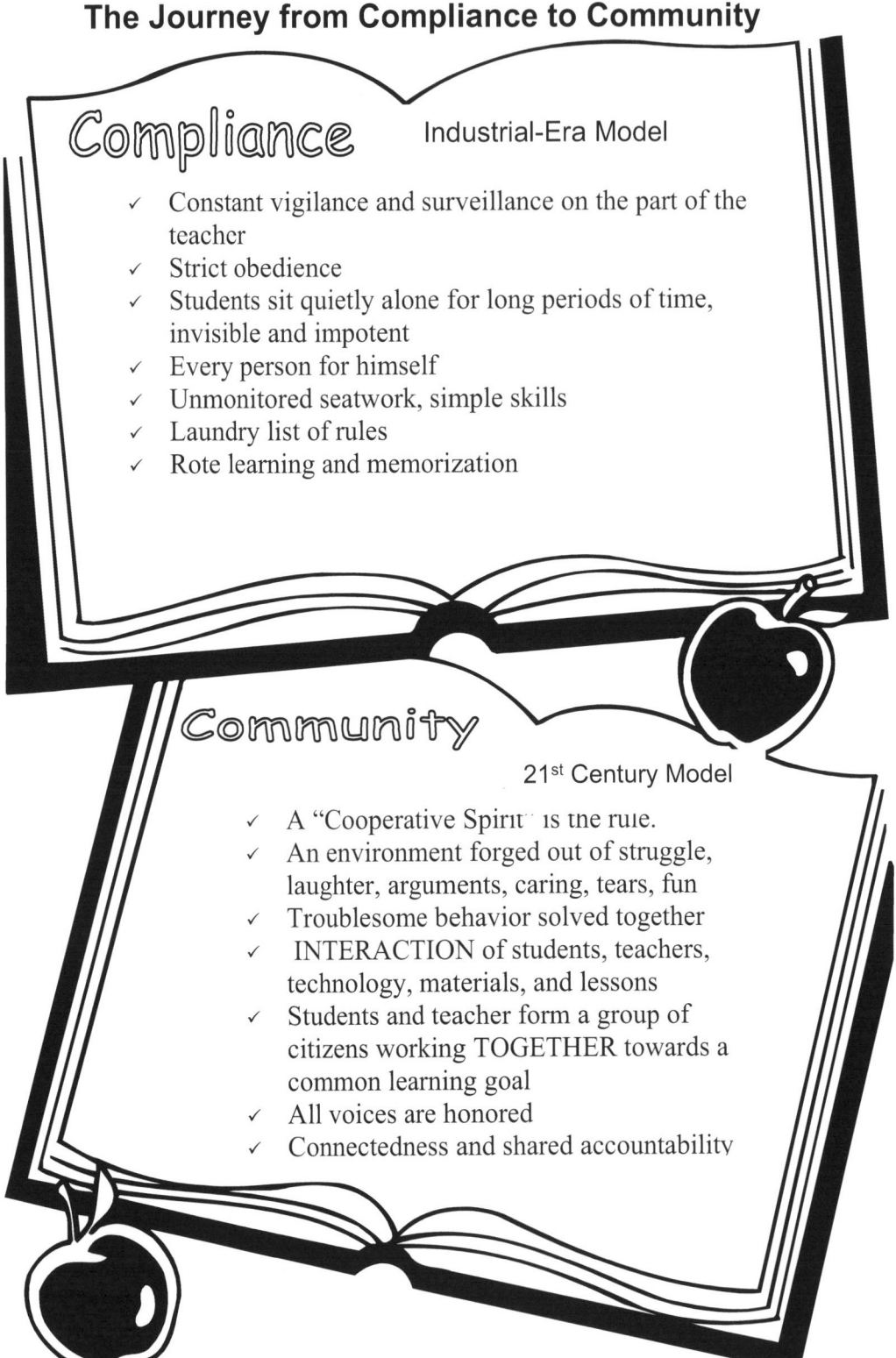

Compliance   Industrial-Era Model

- ✓ Constant vigilance and surveillance on the part of the teacher
- ✓ Strict obedience
- ✓ Students sit quietly alone for long periods of time, invisible and impotent
- ✓ Every person for himself
- ✓ Unmonitored seatwork, simple skills
- ✓ Laundry list of rules
- ✓ Rote learning and memorization

Community

21st Century Model

- ✓ A "Cooperative Spirit" is the rule.
- ✓ An environment forged out of struggle, laughter, arguments, caring, tears, fun
- ✓ Troublesome behavior solved together
- ✓ INTERACTION of students, teachers, technology, materials, and lessons
- ✓ Students and teacher form a group of citizens working TOGETHER towards a common learning goal
- ✓ All voices are honored
- ✓ Connectedness and shared accountability

The Journey from Compliance to Community

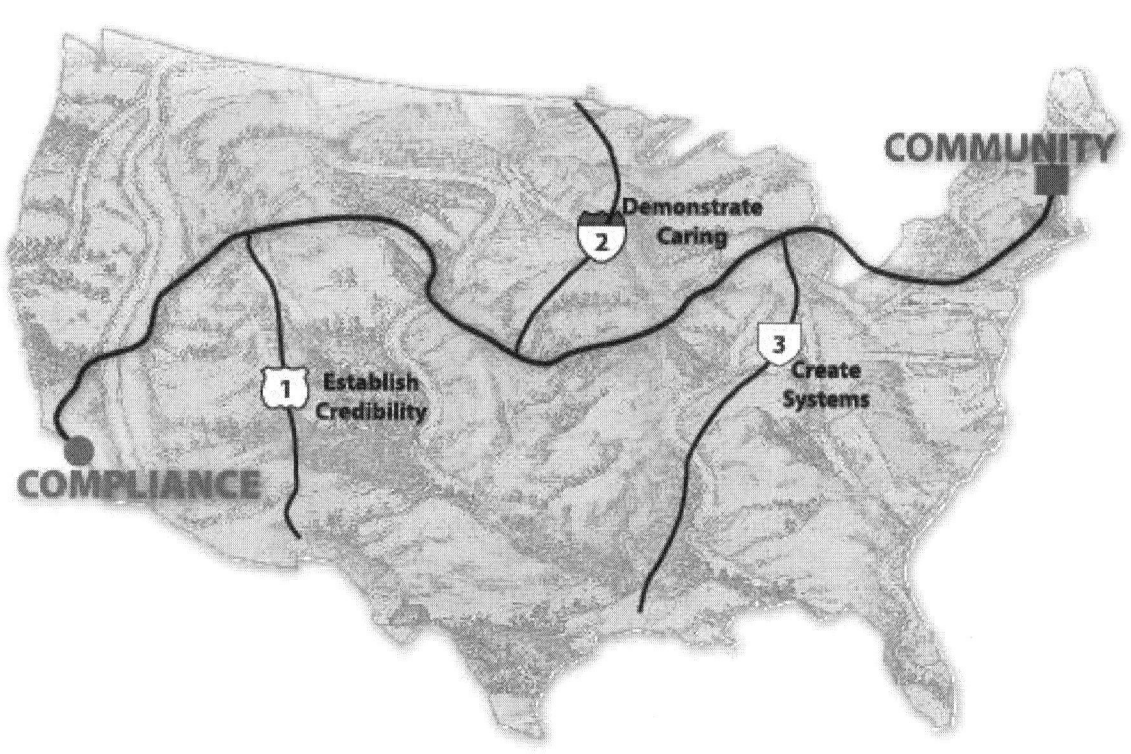

The Owl Mountain Coaching Asset-Mapping System

Discovering and uncovering the collective brilliance of our teachers!

The Asset Mapping System:

Empowering Coaches to Impact Teacher Quality

"Empires of the future are empires of the mind."— A Prescient Winston Churchill

Once upon a time, when we were a farming society, wealth or assets were based on the amount of crops and land owned. When we moved to a smokestack or industrial society, wealth was based on hard, tangible assets: machines, steel furnaces, assembly lines, inventory, equipment. Now with the ascent of the global economy, the meaning of wealth is again being transformed. According to Alvin Toffler's *PowerShift*, we have moved from wealth based on hard assets to the "ideas crackling inside the head of employees… Knowledge cleverly used can generate even more knowledge."

Traditionally, in education, we tend to focus on deficits and gaps, which is a needs-based model of assessment. Too many schools have an **achievement gap or a knowledge deficit**. Teachers, the greatest human capital for improving student achievement, are viewed as unsatisfactory or as liabilities. However, an asset-mapping approach assumes that all actors in a community possess assets (wealth) that they can share with others and build relationships. By identifying and analyzing teachers' beliefs, skills, and capacities, the school and teachers are empowered to leverage the collective assets in order to move past current levels of performance (McKnight and Kretzmann, 2005). By taking stock of and focusing on strengths instead of only on deficiencies, all are afforded an opportunity to share, to shine, and to prosper. Thus, reducing teacher attrition in the school.

The Owl Mountain Coaching Asset-Mapping System™ focuses on the "inner game" of teaching and frames the discussion/conversation about teacher quality and classroom practices. It is a job-embedded, ongoing, formative assessment model that will make all educational programs in the school run better. It is an efficient and replicable model for change (reform/transformation) that enables all in the school or district to be on the same page.

Owl Mountain Coaching Asset Mapping System™:

✓ Is a powerful and unique approach that enables a collaborative "journey" to collect information on teacher quality and classroom practices.

✓ Pinpoints eighteen principles in three core areas critical to teacher and classroom quality, empowering the coach/teacher leader to support new and marginal teachers and to embrace and develop potential teacher leaders.

✓ Identifies existing and lacking assets (teacher strengths and deficits), which equip the coach/leadership team to establish and set quantifiable goals that can be aligned with the School Improvement Plan.

✓ Is an internally focused strategy that promotes school capacity and ownership of the school's greatest human capital for improving student achievement. The approach allows acknowledgement and affirmation of the assets (strengths) within the school that can be leveraged for teachers to support one another and build a professional learning community.

The "journey" begins at a place called "compliance" and ends at a destination named "community." During three "stops" on the journey, eighteen principles in three core areas critical to teacher quality and classroom practices are examined—all keys to a successful classroom environment.

You will be able to identify the highly effective teachers who:

Stop   1   Establish Credibility (Six Guiding Principles)

Stop   2   Demonstrate Caring (Six Guiding Principles)

Stop   3   Create Systems: Rituals and Routines (Six Guiding Principles)

Owl Mountain Coaching Asset-Mapping System™ Process Chart

System: A set of interconnected components working together to fulfill a designated need: **Teacher Quality and Classroom Practices.**
A consistently applied system will beat a non-system.

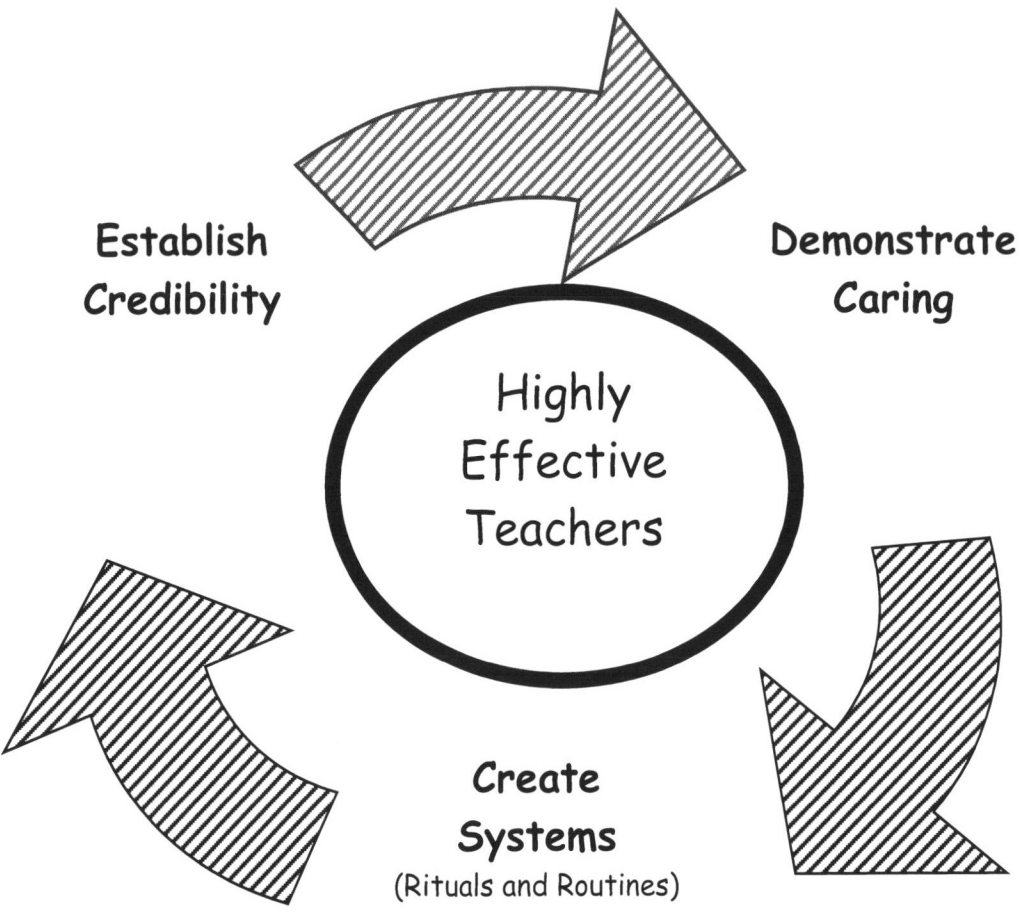

Establish Credibility

Demonstrate Caring

Highly Effective Teachers

Create Systems (Rituals and Routines)

The Schema/Mental Model of Highly Effective Community Builders

Schema: "…the innate structures, which organize our world."

Immanuel Kant,
Eighteenth century philosopher

Schema Theory—process by which we add to (assimilate) or adjust (accommodate) our existing cognitive structure in face of new, familiar, or discordant (radically different) information. (Readence, Bean, Baldwin)

Schema (ta)—organized knowledge structure; includes attitudes, feelings, beliefs; category or system of the mind containing information about the surrounding environment; a central guidance system. A script, frame, scene, scenario, model, mental representation.

It's been said that ninety percent of teaching is from the neck up.

Schema Goal: To bridge teachers' existing knowledge about community-building with new knowledge.

The concept of community is a powerful infrastructure.

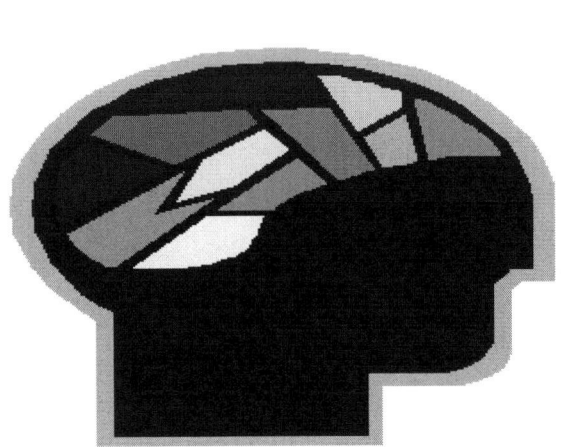

Establish Credibility, Demonstrate Caring, and Create Systems.

The Owl Mountain Coaching Asset-Mapping System Principles™

Principles: Important underlying laws required in a system of thought; basic assumptions, fundamental beliefs standards, truths.

1.0 Establish Credibility

1.1 Teachers create stability as well as credibility because their attendance is better than the district average.

1.2 Teachers dress for success. Each day they dress as if they are going to the workplace.

1.3 Teachers' voices are clear and confident rather than weak and barely audible.

1.4 Teachers' nonverbal body language demonstrates a positive, confident bearing rather than one that is unsure or easily intimidated.

1.5 Teachers' *general* temperament exhibits patience and understanding rather than anger and frustration.

1.6 Teachers exhibit "WITHITNESS." They are aware of classroom surroundings, happenings and students' actions at ALL times. (Jacob Kounin coined the term)

2.0 Demonstrate Caring

2.1 Teachers know and can call ALL of their students by name.

2.2 Teachers are aware that community is people with whom we share our stories, promoting a sense of belonging. Students engage in bonding or getting to know you activities.

2.3   Teachers circulate to **assist** and to **insist** that students work rather than constantly sit at their desks. A "we" are in this together attitude prevails.

2.4   Teachers create bulletin boards that display students' work and promote a caring but rigorous learning environment.

2.5   Teachers are aware of the interpersonal dynamics in my classroom. They have a seating plan in place that creates stability and community.

2.6   Teachers promote a classroom community where students work collaboratively *ependence and individual accountability.*

3.0 Create Systems

3.1   Teachers have developed a syllabus that outlines the framework for success from the beginning of the school year through the end.

3.2   Teachers have rituals/routines in place that make good use of time at the beginning of the period, the end (closure) of the period, precluding a loss of instructional time.

3.3   Teachers require and MONITOR that students bring a notebook and folder to class EACH day because they are crucial to the learning process.

3.4   Teachers give comprehensive midterm assessments and comprehensive final assessments because learning is cumulative (state-mandated tests are based on comprehensive knowledge and skills).

3.5   Teachers' system for assessment (grading) is rarely challenged by students, parents, or the office because it is public, consistent, and ongoing. Students understand their strength/improvement areas and can compute their grades on their own.

3.6   Teachers have a discipline approach/plan in place that is firm, fair, and consistent. They seldom send students to the office.

Welcome New Recruits!

Do you have what it takes to become an effective educator?

New Recruits and Community Building

Before beginning the asset mapping process (pg. 46) for the school, department, or grade level, lay the foundation with this activity.

Goals:

Coaches will analyze and reflect on how highly effective teachers build a high-performance learning community.

Teachers will begin to explore and to share with new "recruits" a personal vision building a high performing classroom community.

Suggested Reading

To build your coaching schema, read these previews about the meaning and importance of community by Peter Block (*Community: The Structure of Belonging*) and Robert Putnam (*Bowling Alone: The Collapse and Revival of the American Community*) before getting started with this activity. They will add to your schema about the importance of community in the twenty-first century. The readings may encourage you to purchase the books, as did I.

http://tinyurl.com/y96hysp Overview of Peter Block's work

www.progressivewomensalliance.org/images/2009_04.pdf Peter Block

http://www.bowlingalone.com/ Robert Putnam

Materials:

Handouts on next pages

Giant and small Post-its

Name tags/plates

Time:

60 to 90 minutes

Audience:

Whole Faculty

New or marginal teachers

Grade-level teams

Content area teams

Coaching Support

What relationships or alliances do you need to build in order to make this activity successful? Highly effective teachers? Leadership team? A virtual professional learning community (VPLC)? How will you document the results of this activity?

Introduction/Gaining Entry

If this is your first meeting with the staff, think about how you want to introduce yourself. Will a staff member introduce you? What do you want him to say? What will you say about yourself? This is your opportunity to break the ice and "establish credibility" or gain entry.

Planning the Activity/Suggestions

What norms or protocols need to be put into place?

Seating: Arrange the meeting space and seating to promote "an equal voice and an equal regard". Seating that promotes eye contact builds community (Peter Block, 2008). Share the background information/conversation.

Parking Lot: You may choose to not answer questions in the middle of delivering a presentation, especially if you are operating under time restraints. Put in place a "question parking lot" where participants can post their questions minimizing interruptions and ensuring all legitimate questions are answered.

Charting/Gallery Walk: Ask groups to chart their responses on a giant Post-it. A great way to share information with the whole group and a great resource for typing up what transpired or was accomplished, it is documentation that can be entered into a wiki or as a pdf on the school's website.

Distribute and read the profiles of the new urban educators on the next pages. Provide time for teachers to respond to the questions individually and as a group. How will you share and document the results of this activity. Where will the documentation reside?

Background

New Teachers Are Coming to Education
Through a Variety of Paths

Because we have entered a Darwinian era and education is one of the few arenas with a built-in budget in the form of a per-pupil allotment, public schools face fierce competition from those who believe we should harness the power of free markets to solve education's problems. College graduates from all sectors now eye schools as a marketplace, seeing them as a lifeline in an economy that is sinking.

Young, energetic students graduate from Ivy League colleges or at the top of their graduating class and decide to teach until the economy improves. A downsized finance expert from the auto industry knows she can teach math. A former police lieutenant believes he can operate a school. An ex-CEO is convinced he can manage a school district. Ex-movers and shakers from the auto industry, government, Silicon Valley, and Wall Street want a piece of the education pie.

However, despite credentials, certification, and scholarship, teaching is also about building a high-performance classroom community, which these new recruits must be able to do if they are to succeed and not contribute to the attrition statistics.

Added Conversation: Integrate your experience and expertise to share with teachers. You may want to change the names in the activity on the next page to suit your context.

Welcome New Recruits

Situation: Eight new recruits (seven teachers and one administrator) are joining the staff for the upcoming school year. Though they may be exemplary in their scholarship, they need to be able to create a community that empowers students to feel part of something larger than themselves. What advice can you give to them?

	New Urban Educators	Subject
1	Colin Powell – Former Secretary of State	Government instructor and JROTC Mentor
2	Toni Morrison- Writer and Nobel Prize Winner for Literature	English instructor and Journalism Advisor
3	Michael Jordan – Former Chicago Bulls' All Star	PE instructor and Basketball Coach
4	Former Surgeon General Dr. David Hatcher	Science instructor and STEM sponsor
5	Bernard Bernanke Secretary of the Federal Reserve	Math instructor and Academic Games Coach
6	Bill Gates, Microsoft Founder, Philanthropist	Computer and Robotics instructor
7	Dr. Phil McGraw –Psychologist	Counselor and student fitness guru.
8	Sarah Palin, Former candidate for vice-president, former governor, politician, activist	Principal/Chancellor/Academy Director

New Educators Join Martin Luther King, Jr. Senior High

Our new educators have passed the National Teachers Examination and are considered qualified, according to No Child Left Behind.

- ❏ What does it mean to build a classroom community that fosters accountability, connectedness, and learning?

- ❏ What advice will you give on how a teacher should establish credibility with students and parents?

- ❏ What advice will you give on demonstrating care by building a rigorous classroom with a heart?

- ❏ What advice will you give on how to create the systems and routines needed to operate their classrooms and build community?

You may want to give advice to the entire group or focus your efforts on one newcomer.

- ⬥ What words of wisdom do you have for the new principal/academy director about teacher quality and classroom practices at the school? How can she work to reduce teacher attrition?

School Culture and Community Building

School culture, an invisible, intangible force, forges the attitudes, beliefs, and values within a school. It is the daily way of life. School culture, anchored by the principal or other school leaders, communicates the collective possibilities—or focuses only on the here and the now. It expresses collegiality and collaborative problem-solving ("We're in this ship together") or "I can't worry about next week; I'm trying to get through today." Culture communes and imparts through verbal and nonverbal body language that we are of one spirit, one heart, or "Just keep the ship afloat; don't let it sink. We won't worry about creativity or innovation; after all, we are teaching in a perfect storm of high poverty, high crime, and high foreclosure rates."

It's whether or not a school has a celebrated choir, a winning sports team, an engaged student government, celebrations, ceremonies, and something for everyone or only the elite and chosen few. School culture instills a sense of community that says, "I belong and I can dream here," or "I am invisible and don't matter."

It's a school that screams: mediocrity, inertia, and entrenched practices, or beams: clean, safe, and orderly. It impacts teachers' efficacy, students' self-beliefs, AND graduation rates.

School culture is a collective human capital that has created a map of the future, a justification for living, or is a human capital breakdown that smells of alienation, disorientation, and dysfunction because no one knows the right thing to do or wants to do what has to be done (Dr. Howard Gardener, et al, *Good Work: When Ethics and Excellence Meet,* 2001).

School culture influences the ability to impact teacher quality and classroom practices.

*P. S   Reread the passage; substitute the term **brand** for the term **culture**. In a 21st century innovation-based, global economy, some reformers insist that schools are a product. Thus, the success of the product is influenced by its **brand**.*

Owl Mountain Coaching Personal Challenge Two

Journal Entry: From Compliance to Community

"Writing holds us responsible for our words and ultimately makes us more thoughtful human beings." Ernest Boyer

In Community: The Structure of Belonging, Peter Block provides various definitions for the term community, among them:
- It's any group that has something in common.
- Communities are built from assets and gifts and not from deficiencies and needs.
- Change the culture; change the community.
- Communities are places where people want to show up.
- Collegiality promotes community.

✓ After completing the Welcome New Recruits activity, what have you learned about how teachers in your school view community? Are you in accord? Why or why not?

✓ Based on the definitions above, Is the school in which you work a community? What proof do you have that the school is or is not a community?

✓ What impact will the concept of community have on teacher attrition and student achievement in this school?

✓ Informally, begin to visit the classrooms. Does it "feel" of community? Do they need to "journey" from compliance to community? If so, what will you do about it?

*Have you identified a **trusted peer** to share the insights from your journal?*

Notes

"We don't receive wisdom; we must discover it for ourselves after a journey that no one can take for us or spare us." Marcel Proust

Consistent, predictable results
require a common language.

Getting Started with Asset Mapping

Asset-Mapping Goals:

The coach/teacher leader will:

- Research and increase his background knowledge about the concept of asset-mapping.
- Assist teachers with identifying their beliefs, skills, strengths (assets).
- Assist teachers with Identifying their underdeveloped and undeveloped assets.
- Chart teachers' beliefs, skills, strengths.
- Differentiate between the concepts of compliance and community.
- Plan with teachers to create their unique teaching profile (see Appendix A).
- Determine how teachers can collaborate and build relationships.

Suggested Readings

Before getting started with the asset-mapping activity, you may want to preview these two links. They will fill your background knowledge about the concept of asset mapping:
http://www.abcdinstitute.org/ The Asset-Based Community Development Institute at Northwestern University
http://www.abcdinstitute.org/publications/basicmanual/

Materials:

Giant Post-it notepad and markers

A copy of the principles for each teacher

Giant Post-it or flip chart

Who is the audience for this activity?
- ✓ Whole staff meetings
- ✓ Content or grade-level meetings
- ✓ One-on-one teacher support
- ✓ Parent meetings

Coaching Support:

What relationships or alliances do you need to build in order to make this activity successful? Highly effective teachers? The leadership team? A virtual professional learning community (VPLC)?

Maintenance:

Because this is a formative assessment activity, what follow-through is necessary?

Time:

Minimum 60 to 90 minutes for each core area

Instructions:

Seating: Encourage teachers to sit in groups of four or more, facing one another. Recommend that they sit with others who teach in their content area or grade level.

Review the three core areas from the Welcome New Recruits icebreaker if time has passed since the start of this activity.

Distribute ONE set of guiding principles at a time.

At each "stop" on the journey, encourage teachers to **collaborate** with their peers to complete their individual asset map/survey, identifying their areas of strength and areas for growth (undeveloped or underdeveloped assets).

Transfer these attributes onto the chart on the next page or on the Plan of Action Sheets (see Unique Teaching Profile in Appendix A).

Encourage teachers to write their own "conversations" to share with the group.

The initial mapping (formative) provides a baseline to measure progress over time. Asset mapping aggregates the knowledge possessed by individual teachers or teams of teachers, allowing us to widen the classroom keyhole to see and to understand what highly effective teachers are doing in their classrooms. Those who exhibit strong skills and capacities in the core areas can serve as models for those teachers who are less effective in those areas. Working together enhances career longevity, reducing teacher attrition.

Documenting Assets Process Chart

Grade Level   Content Area

Core Area: Establish Credibility, or Demonstrate Caring, or Create Systems		
Principle No.	Assets (Strengths)	Assets: Undeveloped, Underdeveloped

Core Area:
Highly Effective Teachers Establish Credibility 1.0

Asset Mapping Teacher Quality: Building a
school culture that says this is how we do
business despite who comes or goes!

Highly Effective Teachers Establish Credibility
Journey Stop 1.0

"Credibility is like virginity. Once you lose it..."
—Unknown

As CEO of the classroom community, the teacher builds his brand through his credibility, which is communicated in diverse ways. In order to persuade students, the clients, that the content is valuable and worth learning, the teacher must be perceived as not only intelligent and knowledgeable, but as trustworthy, reliable, strong, fair, and wise. Imparted through attendance, dress, voice, nonverbal body language, and intuition, credibility promotes/supports the teacher's ability to construct a classroom community of social growth and joint intellectual effort. Credentials and certification help provide credence that the teacher is an expert in his field; however, highly effective teachers know that there's more. Credibility inspires students to believe in and feel that they can learn from the teacher. The success of both the teacher's and the students' school year depends on establishing credibility.

Added Conversation: Integrate your experience and expertise to share with teachers. Do you want to include a professional learning community in this activity? Have you Established Credibility with the staff?

Notes

"We don't receive wisdom; we must discover it for ourselves after a journey that no one can take for us or spare us." Marcel Proust

Owl Mountain Principles

CONVERSATIONS
WITH A
COACH

Dear Teacher, How Do You Establish Credibility?

Reflect on the principles listed below. What principles can you teach or share with others (assets)? What are your areas for growth: undeveloped or underdeveloped? In the blank space, write a conversation/comment to share with a coach or other trusted professional. **Do your students see you as credible? How do you know?**

An Asset	Underdeveloped Asset	Undeveloped Asset

1.1   I create stability as well as credibility because my attendance is better than the school average.

1.2   I dress for success. Each day I dress as if I am going to the workplace.

1.3   My teaching voice is clear and confident rather than weak and barely audible.

1.4   My nonverbal body language demonstrates a positive, confident bearing rather than one that is unsure or easily intimidated.

1.5.   My general temperament exhibits patience and understanding rather than anger and frustration.

1.6.   I exhibit "WITHITNESS." I am aware of classroom surroundings, happenings and students' actions at ALL times. (Jacob Kounin coined the term.)

Write/journal: Create a vision statement for establishing credibility with your students. What are your "inner assets"?

Conversations for the Journey

Dear Coach,

As you begin to navigate *The Journey from Compliance to Community* with teachers, the sample "conversations" on the next pages will help you find and strengthen your "voice" during the tough spots.

Modify or edit what I have written to suit your situation. Integrate YOUR insights about how highly effective teachers establish credibility. These "conversations" will build your schema. Think of them as a starting point.

How will you document which teachers have established credibility? How will you pair them with others?

Lorraine Richardson, Chief Owl

P.S. Have you joined a professional learning community: virtual or face-to-face?

1.0 Establishing Credibility

"When an archer misses the mark, he turns and looks for the fault within himself. Failure to hit the bulls'-eye is never the fault of the target. To improve your aim, improve yourself."

—*Gilbert Ariand*

Guiding Principle 1.1 Teachers create stability as well as credibility because their attendance is better than the district average **(school culture)**.

The importance of sheer physical presence cannot be overestimated. At-risk kids need extra time, extra energy, and extra focus that can only be achieved with showing up on a daily basis. Being considered reliable, dependable, and consistent by students promotes the security and stability they need to learn.

Added Comments/Conversations: Integrate your experience and expertise.

Guiding Principle 1.2: Teachers dress for success. Each day they dress as if they are going to the workplace (*school culture*).

Many students may have no role model at home or in their lives for a suitable workplace dress code. Also, students see and respond to fashion. Is yours conservative or outrageous? Is your mid-drift showing, or is your top cut low? Are your pants too tight or too short (floods)? Does your hairstyle or hair length detract from the lesson? Are your nails long and curved? Do you "sport" a disheveled, rough-dried appearance?

Added Comments/Conversations: Integrate your experience and expertise. Do you anticipate opposition from the teacher?

Guiding Principle 1.3: Most teachers' voices are clear and confident rather than weak and barely audible.

Like a musical instrument capable of spanning a wide range of moods and emotions, the teaching voice can convey happiness, frustration, trust, doubt, faith, anger, or sadness. When we were children and our parents called us, we could tell by their tone how fast we should respond. We can teach students to respond to us in the same manner. Used effectively, the voice demonstrates our confidence that students' success is possible and probable.

Added Comments/Conversations: Integrate your experience and expertise.

Guiding Principle 1.4: Most teachers' nonverbal body language demonstrates a positive, confident bearing rather than one that is unsure or easily intimidated.

The voice and body language work collaboratively to communicate our mental and emotional state to students. Facial expression shows approval or disapproval. Eye contact says that I am in control—"Don't trespass because I am the authority." Seating an unruly student near you (physical proximity) or standing near one generally causes misbehavior to cease. No words are necessary.

Success begins with believing success is possible. Positive body language announces, "I'm courageous, strong, and wise. It's okay to lean on me because I will catch you if you fall or make a mistake."

Added Comments/Conversations: Integrate your experience and expertise.

Guiding Principle 1.5: The teacher's (daily) general **temperament** exhibits patience and understanding rather than anger and frustration.

A frustrated voice and tight body language exhibit, "I am not certain that I can teach you this material. I don't understand why everyone doesn't know this by now." Students take their cue from the teacher as to whether or not they are able to master the subject or whether or not the teacher is competent and capable of teaching it. Credibility is enhanced or detracted by temperament.

Added Comments/Conversations: Integrate your experience and expertise.

Guiding Principle 1.6: Teachers exhibit "WITHITNESS." They are aware of classroom surroundings, happenings, and students' actions at ALL times—**the *Art* of teaching.**

"WITHITNESS," said to be the **art of teaching**, rather than the science of teaching, means the teacher is aware of what's going on in the classroom at ALL times. Do you have "eyes in the back of your head"? The term was coined by Jacob Kounin.

Added Comments/Conversations: Integrate your experience and expertise.

How will you advocate and rally support
for your efforts as a coach?

Establish Credibility-
Asset Building Activities 1.0

The Teaching Voice and Body Language

The Owl Mountain Coaching ™ Asset Building Activities on the following pages are aligned with the core area, establishing credibility. The activities contain principles that effective teachers practice intuitively at an unconscious level, much like an outstanding athlete who is "in the zone," executing plays without being able to explain why or how. With your patience and staying power, these activities will encourage in-depth exchange about teacher quality.

The voice is like a musical instrument,
sometimes sweet and sometimes harsh!

The Teaching Voice and Body Language Increase Credibility

Guiding Principle 1.3 : My teaching voice is clear and confident rather than weak and barely audible.

Guiding Principle 1.4: My **nonverbal body language** demonstrates a positive, confident bearing rather than one that is unsure or easily intimidated.

Guiding Principle 1.5: My *general temperament* exhibits patience and understanding rather than anger and frustration.

Goals
The coach will:
- Work with teachers to analyze the critical attributes of the "teaching voice" and the nonverbal message.
- Support teachers in their efforts to develop a "teaching voice."
- Assist teachers with aligning the teaching voice with their nonverbal body language.
- Discuss how the teaching voice and body language impact student behavior and communicate expectations.

Materials
Script/conversations and activities on the next pages
A web cam, phone camera, or any device that will allow teachers to record their voice and/or videotape their teaching.

Time
This taping activity should be performed and repeated over a period of mutually agreed-upon time intervals.
If teachers are hesitant about your videotaping their lessons, encourage them to start alone by audio taping their lessons over a period of two weeks.

How will you select the audience for this activity?
- ✓ New teachers?
- ✓ Teachers with poor classroom management?
- ✓ Self-selection? Nomination?

Coaching Support:
What relationships or alliances do you need to build in order to make this activity successful? Highly effective teachers who exhibit an exemplary teaching voice and the accompanying body language? Leadership team? Virtual Professional Learning Community?

Maintenance:
Because this is a formative assessment activity, what kind of follow-up will be necessary?

Instructions:
Create videos and upload them to an intranet or other private site for critiquing.
Share the background information.
Complete the "conversations" with selected audience.
Request that teachers share several recordings with you and/or a group of their peers.
Have them complete the Voice Assessment activity at mutually agreed-upon intervals.
Work with them to establish goals.

Background/Conversation

Like a musical instrument, the teaching voice is capable of a variety of emotions and must be used judiciously to avoid fatigue. The vocal tones—anger, frustration, impatience—are like strong spices that should be used lightly.

Your voice determines your belief in your students and your belief in you. Many times we communicate to students through our tone of voice that we care about them, **are afraid of them**, or *lack confidence* in our ability to teach them.

- ✓ A **confident voice** displays, "I have the ability to teach this material and I believe you can learn it."
- ✓ A **frustrated voice** reveals, "I am not certain that I can teach you this material. I don't understand why everyone doesn't know this by now."

So much of behavior management depends on the voice and body language.

Effective teachers, like effective public speakers, engage their audiences. Because the act of teaching requires enormous concentration, we may not always be aware of everything we say or how we say it. That is why I recommend that you tape your voice over a period of months.

Added Comments/Conversations: Integrate your experience and expertise. What, if any opposition, do you anticipate from teachers?

Reflective Conversations

- Describe a time when your tone of voice made a difference, either a positive or a negative difference in a student's life.
- What internalized knowledge do you have about your voice?
- Are you aware of how your voice communicates your outer state/nonverbal body language?
- What does body language involve?
- How much of effective classroom behavior management depends on tone of voice and body language?
- Why is it said that effective body language or facial expressions are worth 1,000 words?
- Have you ever stared a student down? How did it feel?

CONVERSATIONS WITH A COACH

An angry tone puts out the fire. Occasionally, it is effective because it means that there is the devil to pay.

Teaching Voice Assessment

Objective: To audio- and/or videotape several lessons for the purpose of assessing the voice/teaching tone.

1. My general tone lacks confidence.
A. No problem   B. Sometimes   C. Needs improvement

2 My general tone is barely audible.
A. No problem   B. Sometimes   C. Needs improvement

3 My general tone is argumentative/confrontational.
A. No problem   B. Sometimes   C. Needs improvement

4 My general tone is angry, negative.
A. No problem   B. Sometimes   C. Needs improvement

5 My general tone is loud.
A. No problem   B. Sometimes   C. Needs improvement

6 My tone is pleasing and calm.
A. No problem   B. Sometimes   C. Needs improvement

7. I dominate the lesson with "teach talk" (I talk too much).
A. No problem   B. Sometimes   C. Needs improvement

8. My general tone of voice lacks firmness.
A. No problem   B. Sometimes   C. Needs improvement

9. Students respond to my voice.
A. No problem   B. Sometimes   C. Needs improvement

10. Students can determine when I mean business.
A. No problem   B. Sometimes   C. Needs improvement

Verbal Assessment—Enunciation and Distracting Fillers

Pronouncing each word clearly, distinctly, and correctly reinforces your credibility as a teacher and as a professional.

Which, if any, distracting fillers do you use?

Distraction	Correction	Growth Area?
You know, uh, for sure, you see, like etc.	ELIMINATE THEM	
Wanna gunna	Want to ; going to	
Yur	Your	
Wouldja, couldja	Would you, could you	
Fur	For	
Kin	Can	
Mondey; Tuesdey	Monday, Tuesday, etc	
Git	Get	
Ta	To	
Hunderd	hundred	

Goal Setting: *The Teaching Voice*

The voice is a most important tool in establishing credibility in the classroom.

TM

What conversation do you want to hold about the teacher's verbal skills? How do you articulate your concerns succinctly, clearly, and diplomatically? What conflict-free script can you write to support him on the "journey"?

Who are the models in the school that can serve as a positive example? Listed below are reflective questions you might want to use with the teacher.

1.   As a result of listening to your voice, what conclusions can you draw about your teaching tone?

2.   Is your body language aligned with your teaching voice? Describe your overall teaching energy. Is it calm, assertive, nervous? Explain.

3.   Identify your area(s) for growth.

4.   How long does growth take?

The Teaching Voice Outside of the Classroom
(Schools with Security Guards, Take Note!)

Objective: To use the voice as a tool for securing cooperation while on hall duty or in the student cafeteria, or anywhere in the school other than the classroom.

While on hall duty, it is often necessary to make requests of students with whom we have developed no relationship. It is not like being in the classroom, where we know students' names and we exhibit varying degrees of control.

In attempting NOT to be confrontational with students in the hall and, thereby, not lose control of the situation, we should approach students with a firm but non-confrontational tone, referring to them as "young man," "sir," "young lady," or "miss" if we do not know their names. In addition, the use of "please" and "thank you" when making requests increases cooperation.

EXAMPLES

"**Sir, thank you** for picking up that popcorn that you just spilled; I appreciate it very much."

"**Young lady**, where is your pass? You are in violation of the Student Code of Conduct (or whatever the student discipline code is called in your district)."

"**Young man**, please refrain from…"

(**NEVER** call an African-American teenage male "boy.")

Keep **repeating** the request in a firm tone (do not plead or beg) until you gain cooperation. Using this approach lets the students know that we are the voice of reason and authority, but we care because we are giving respect by addressing them in a positive manner.

The Teaching Voice

"I have come to the conclusion that I am the decisive element in the classroom. As a teacher, I possess tremendous power to make a child's life miserable or joyous. I can be a tool of torture or an instrument of inspiration. I can humiliate or humor, hurt or heal. In all situations, it is my response (voice) that decides whether a crisis will be escalated or de-escalated, and a child humanized or dehumanized."

Haim Ginott, Psychologist

The Coaching Voice

In the quote above, substitute the word "teacher" with the word "coach" and substitute the word "child" with the word "teacher."

Owl Mountain Coaching Personal Challenge Three

Journal Entry: Honoring All Voices

"Writing holds us responsible for our words and ultimately makes us more thoughtful human beings." Ernest Boyer

Coaches need to be highly skilled and sensitive listeners with superior oral communication skills. It is crucial that you master the verbal and the nonverbal message.

- ✓ Have you examined your voice? Is is threatening or soothing? Is it confident or arrogant? Do you cut others with your eye contact and tongue, or do you display a non-threatening, nonjudgmental face and tone? How do you know? Have you ever taped a conversation with a teacher?

- ✓ What part does your voice and body language play in asking teachers to examine or change their practice?

- ✓ As the coach, there may be times you will be duty-bound to tell teachers what they need to hear rather than what they want to hear. How will you use your voice and body language to navigate that process?

*Have you identified a **trusted peer** to share the insights from your journal?*

Notes

"We don't receive wisdom; we must discover it for ourselves after a journey that no one can take for us or spare us." Marcel Proust

\

Dear Coach,
How are you chronicling and sharing your challenges,
insights, solutions, strategies, and wins?

Core Area:
Highly Effective Teachers
Demonstrate Caring
2.0

United we stand; divided we fall.
We sink or swim together.

Highly Effective Teachers Demonstrate Caring:

Building a Rigorous Classroom Community with a Heart

Journey Stop 2.0

"I don't care how much you know until I know how much you care."
—Mother Teresa

Demonstrating care requires designing a classroom community that makes students feel wanted, loved, and cared for. Teachers are surrogate parents, objects of affection, and objects of anger who are charged with demonstrating care by constructing a classroom with a heart. A rigorous but caring classroom community supports social capital: belonging, friendship, camaraderie—a connection among students as they attempt to translate their aspirations into realities (http://www.bowlingalone.com/).

The age of globalization has created a human connectedness that is more fragile than ever. Because technology has redefined time and distance, and we now build community through virtual social networks, we have become disconnected from face-to-face relationships; our interdependence has plunged. Seating students in single rows only reinforces this disconnectedness and promotes an "every student for himself" atmosphere. Face-to-face learning, which reduces the invisibility and impotence insidious in so many urban classrooms, allows intellectual discussion to become a natural activity, sometimes friendly and sometimes not (the new dinner table).

Highly effective teachers understand that demonstrating care requires creating a rich, rigorous community that structures belonging and builds relatedness, a community where students feel: "I am safe, among friends, and my voice is honored" (Peter Strong, *Community: The Structure of Belonging).*

Added Conversation: Integrate your experience and expertise to share with teachers. How will you demonstrate caring as a coach?

Notes

"We don't receive wisdom; we must discover it for ourselves after a journey that no one can take for us or spare us." Marcel Proust

Owl Mountain Principles

Dear Teacher, How Do You Demonstrate Caring?

CONVERSATIONS
WITH A
COACH

     Reflect on the principles listed below. What principles can you teach or share with others (assets)? What are your areas for growth: undeveloped or underdeveloped? In the blank space, write a conversation/comment to share with a coach/teacher leader other trusted professional. What goals do you need to set?

Asset	**Underdeveloped Asset**	**Undeveloped Asset**

2.1   I know and can call ALL of my students by name.

2.2   I am aware that community is people with whom we share our stories, promoting a sense of belonging. Students engage in bonding or getting to know you activities.

2.3   I circulate to **assist** and to **insist** that students work rather than constantly sit at my desk. A "We" are in this together attitude prevails.

2.4   I create bulletin boards that display students' work and promote a caring but rigorous learning environment.

2.5   I am aware of the interpersonal dynamics in my classroom. I have a seating plan in place that creates stability and community

2.6   I promote a classroom community where students work collaboratively as well as independently: *interdependence and individual accountability.*

Write/journal: Create a vision statement for demonstrating care. Describe your inner assets.

Conversations for the Journey

Dear Coach,

As you navigate *The Journey from Compliance to Community* with teachers, the sample "conversations" on the next pages will help you find your voice during the tough spots.

Modify or edit what I have written to suit your situation. Integrate YOUR insights about how highly effective teachers: demonstrate caring. These "conversations" will build your schema. Think of them as a starting point.

Lorraine Richardson, Chief Owl

P.S. How do you know which teachers demonstrate caring? How will you pair them with others? How can caring promote YOUR career/coaching longevity?

2.0   Demonstrate Caring

Creating the rigorous classroom with a HEART that allows a student to grow socially, emotionally, and academically.

Guiding Principle 2.1: The teachers know and can call ALL of *their* students by name **(school culture).**

Anomie is a sense of rootlessness prevalent in large schools where the possibility of anonymity too often becomes a probability, a certainty. When students are called by name, they are not anonymous; they "belong" (Emile Durkheim, "Father of Sociology"). According to Dale Carnegie, "a person's name is the sweetest and most important sound in any language." It feels good to the student and it makes a connection between the two of you. Think how good it feels when someone walks up to you and remembers your name.

Added Comments/Conversations: Integrate your experience and expertise.

Guiding Principle 2.2: Teachers are aware that community is people with whom we share our stories, promoting a sense of belonging. Students engage in "bonding" or "getting to know you" activities."

Bonding promotes the social aspect of learning and reduces invisibility and impotence felt by so many students. Bonding honors the psyche and builds trust. Don't get started with too much content too soon BEFORE building a community that is teacher-to-student, student-to-teacher, and student-to-student. Community is about co-creating our future through sharing our stories. When students know and understand a classmate's journey, it makes it easier for them to like and to trust one another.

Added Comments/Conversations: Integrate your experience and expertise

Guiding Principle 2.3: The teachers circulate to **assist** and to **insist** that students work rather than constantly sit at their desks. A "we" are in this together attitude prevails **(school culture)**.

This practice has a psychological and social impact on students; a partnership is formed that says WE are in this together. **A HUMAN CARING FACTOR** is involved. A teacher who repeatedly sits at the desk enters into a silent agreement with the class not to challenge one another—a peace-at-any-price agreement to get through each hour of the day, 180+ days a year. (This practice prepared high school students for a life in the factory or for the repetitive routines in an office)

Circulating allows us to send a **nonverbal message** that says, "I want to help you." Teaching on our feet is hands-on teaching that allows the teacher to circulate and recognize mistakes and to correct them. We are better servicing our CLIENTELE by giving knowledge of results immediately: *ALMOST, BETTER QUALITY, NOT ACCEPTABLE.*

We have an opportunity to "put out fires" (disciplinary action) before they have an opportunity to spread (Carol Cummings, *Teachers Make a Difference).* Circulating permits us to cajole, flatter, threaten, push, intimidate, and encourage students to be the **best** that they can be.

Added Comments/Conversations: Integrate your experience and expertise.

Guiding Principle 2.4: The teachers create bulletin boards that display students' work and promote a caring but rigorous learning environment (*school culture*).

Is the classroom a drab, lackluster environment promoting disinterest and apathy on the part of students, or is it a vibrant, colorful place creating a warm feeling, making it a place of promise? When parents, students, or visitors enter your room, can they tell what is being taught in the room by its appearance? How are the wall spaces and bulletin boards utilized in your classroom? How often should bulletin boards be changed? Why should students play any role in their creation or maintenance?

Added Comments/Conversations: Integrate your experience and expertise.

Guiding Principle 2.5: The teachers are aware of the interpersonal dynamics in their classroom. They have seating plans in place that create stability and community **(school culture)**.

A seating **plan** is NOT the same thing as a seating **chart**. There is a huge difference:

- ✓ A seating **plan** becomes "social engineering," a foundation for social, emotional, and intellectual behavior, especially when students sit daily next to peers who can be supportive. A seating **chart** is merely documentation of what might be a random seating arrangement.
- ✓ Diversity requires paying closer attention to seating if students are to acquire the "ethnic sensitivities" required for the new millennium. The twenty-first century workforce mandates people skills necessary to work, live, and learn with others who are increasingly likely to be of a different religious, racial, linguistic, and cultural background (Suarez-Orozco, Qin-Howard, *Globalization: Culture and Education in the New Millennium*).
- ✓ Just as most of us live in a permanent location, students need some semblance of permanence and stability.
- ✓ A seating plan used to call a student by name reduces conflict when a substitute teacher is in the room. Seating plans are an aid in learning students' names faster.

By the end of the first month of school, the dynamics of the class should be apparent and the teacher should have a seating PLAN in place. Until that time, students can be seated alphabetically or where they please with the understanding that this may be a temporary arrangement. The seating plan may be adjusted periodically, but students need to be made aware of the teacher's system.

Added Comments/Conversations: Integrate your experience and expertise.

Guiding Principle 2.6: The teachers are aware of the interconnectedness of humans and promote a classroom community where students work collaboratively as well as independently—interdependence and individual accountability.

A classroom community where students are seated face-to-face and side-by-side advances discussion or "conversations," thus promoting reading to and writing for an authentic audience. Too often we ask students to master concepts, theories, and algorithms that they have never verbalized (brain-based learning). In addition, students learn what they can do collectively; they can later perform independently (Vygotsky).

A classroom community contributes to the common good because it:

- is a "human quilt" of learners.
- honors all voices.
- provides accountability and builds relationships because students have a stake in one another.
- teaches responsibility and justice.

Added Comments/Conversations: Integrate your experience and expertise. What opposition, if any, do you anticipate from teachers about seating students face-to-face?

ANOMIE

Contributing to the Silent Epidemic - Dropping Out!

- Rootlessness, futility, anxiety prevalent in large schools where the possibility of anonymity becomes a probability, a certainty
- A lack of structure, rules, organization
- Social instability caused by erosion of standards and values
- Alienation, disorientation, and purposeless
- School/classroom/institutional disorganization and dysfunction.

—Emile Durkheim,
"Father of Sociology"

"The greatest disease in the West today is not TB or leprosy; it is being unwanted, unloved, and uncared for."—Mother Teresa

"The web of our life is mingled yarn, good and ill together."
—William Shakespeare,
All's Well That Ends Well
Act IV, Scene 3

"A person will self-destruct without a goal."
—Dr. Benjamin Mays,
President of Morehouse College

Demonstrating Care Asset Building Activities 2.0

Demonstrating Care
Classroom Seating: Honoring Social and Intellectual Exchange

The Owl Mountain Coaching ™ Asset-Building activity on the following pages is aligned with the core area, demonstrating care. The activity is a standalone instrument containing principles that effective teachers practice intuitively at an unconscious level, much like an outstanding athlete who is "in the zone," executing plays without being able to explain why or how. With your patience and staying power, this activity will encourage in-depth exchange about teacher quality and classroom practices.

"Dialogue is not a tile in the mosaic called school".

Classroom Seating: Honoring Social and Intellectual Exchange

Demonstrating Care, Guiding Principle 2.2: I am aware that community is people with whom we share our stories, promoting a sense of belonging. Students engage in "bonding" or "getting to know you" activities."

Demonstrating Care, Guiding Principle 2.5: I am aware of the interpersonal dynamics in my classroom. I have a seating plan in place that creates stability, community, and fosters intellectual exchange among students.

Demonstrating Care, Guiding Principle 2.6: I promote a classroom community where students work collaboratively as well as independently: interdependence and individual accountability.

Goals:
The coach/teacher leader will assist teachers:
- Differentiate between a seating chart and a seating plan.
- Analyze the thought process that goes into developing a seating plan.
- Create a caring learning community where dialogue prevails over monologue.
- Explore the need for building a strong, connected classroom community.
- Examine and share bonding activities that help create community.
- Analyze a lesson that melds individual accountability with interdependence.

Materials:
The sheets on the next pages should be duplicated and shared.

Time:
60 to 90 minutes to begin the conversation

Who is the audience for this activity?
- ✓ Staff meetings
- ✓ Content or grade-level meetings
- ✓ One-on-one teacher support
- ✓ Parent meetings

Coaching Support:
What relationships or alliances do you need to build in order to make this activity successful? Highly effective teachers? Leadership team? Virtual Professional Learning Community?

Maintenance:
Because this is a formative assessment activity, what follow-up is necessary?

Instructions:
Review the "conversations" that accompany guiding principles 2.2, 2.5 and 2.6. Encourage teachers to sit face-to-face in small groups, promoting an equal voice and an equal regard.

Opening Question/Activity:
How can you develop a seating arrangement that honors the interconnectedness of humans?
Ask for one participant from each group to share his or her response. Think about how and when you want to share the background information below.

Background Information:
According to Peter Block in *Community: The Structure of Belonging,* physical space is more decisive in creating community than we realize. Most classrooms are designed for power and control by the teacher, designed for one expert to demonstrate and disseminate her expertise. While the room itself is not going to change, teachers always have a choice about how we rearrange and occupy whatever classroom we are assigned. Community is built when we can renounce an environment where a spotlight shines only on a selected few students and can create a space that honors peer-to-peer communication. Therefore, in order to create a classroom based on community, we need to examine our thinking about physical seating arrangements and examine the social dynamics of students in the classroom.

In addition, reading and writing are social acts. We read to discuss and we write to be read. **All teachers** are reading and writing teachers because all students need to be able to read, write, and speak knowledgeably about music, basketball, computers, science, math, government, etc. Reading and writing should be more than jumping through hurdles for a grade. Thus face-to-face seating promotes authentic learning.

During the industrial era, corporations directly or indirectly provided security and stability. Corporate taxes and wages allowed us to experience community and fellowship through religious, social, and fraternal organizations, which, in turn, instilled within us a sense of self, a sense of who we could be if we played by the rules.

No more!

Now our institutions struggle financially and our children suffer because of it. More than ever, the classroom community must compensate for the turmoil in our students' lives by providing an emotionally safe harbor that promotes Intellectual development AND social skills.

Can we build a caring community that creates accountability and relatedness if students cannot make eye contact and face one another?

Added Comments/Conversations: Integrate your experience and expertise. What opposition do you expect from teachers concerning face-to-face seating?

A Small Group or Face-to-Face Seating Arrangement Promotes Synergy. They

1. Promote and value ALL student's' unique beliefs, strengths, skills.
2. Provide opportunities to think through and discuss ideas, information, and problems under peer and teacher guidance.
3. Afford everyone the opportunity to participate in discussion, not just the same five or six students.
4. Furnish a small, authentic audience for reading and writing assignments where students can learn to reflect on and to evaluate their own ideas, and those of others.
5. Create a situation that gives experiences in leading and in following.
6. Provide a support group. Confidence as an individual can be enhanced through success in a group.
7. Provide an opportunity to work effectively in a civil manner with individuals who have different beliefs and/or who come from different cultural backgrounds.

In an environment where students sit face-to-face and are interdependent, student-to-student dialogue is a foundation upon which collaborative learning and accountability are based. Research indicates that through dialogue young people can solve problems they cannot solve working alone (Vygotsky). A humanistic approach to teaching that involves the heart and the mind, face-to-face learning is both person-centered and content-centered. It provides opportunities to work effectively in a civil manner with individuals who have different expertise and/or who come from different cultural backgrounds.

Face-to-Face Seating Suggestions:

✓ Administer an assessment test (if possible, assign one high-needs student, one low-needs and two average-needs students to each group).
✓ Identify motivational levels; mix high, average, and low levels.
✓ Students can be grouped according to **teacher choice**, a mix of religious or cultural diversity, self-choice, alphabetical order, numbering system, at random, academic, and/or motivation level.
✓ A mix of males and females is generally more efficient and effective in a coed classroom.

Children interacting towards a common goal tend to regulate each other's actions. When they work together on complex tasks, they assist each other in the same way adults assist children. They solve difficult problems that they can't solve alone.

Lev Vygotsky
Development theorist and researcher who
influenced the work of collaborative learning

Dear Teacher, Do You Have a Seating Plan?

How can you develop a seating arrangement that honors the accountability and interconnectedness of students, thus creating community? How do you honor the intellectual and social exchange of the learning process?

1. How are the desks/ table and chairs arranged in the classroom? Why? Draw a seating map/plan for your room.

2. What is the difference between a seating chart and a seating plan?

3. How often do students sit face-to-face and side-by-side in order to collaborate? Why?
    A. Daily   B. Weekly   C. Several times a month
    D. Monthly   E. Never

4. What guidelines do you use for your seating plan?

5. How can you create a seating plan that honors learning as social and intellectual?

6. What are some of the challenges of seating students face-to-face and side-by-side? How can they be overcome?

7. Could using a webcam, Skype, or live video streaming be as effective as a face-to-face model of teaching and learning? Why or why not?

Discussion Groups: Synergy, Energy

Suggestions for Getting Started (Teacher Instructions)
Divide students into groups of three or four. Students can be grouped according to teacher choice, self-choice, alphabetical order, numbering system, at random, or motivation level (a mix of males and females is generally more efficient and effective). You might want to administer an assessment test. (Assign one high-needs student, one low-needs, and two average-needs students to each group.)

1. Read the responsibilities for a group leader/facilitator—next pages.
2. Select or have students select a leader/facilitator.
3. Distribute an assignment/prompt to the entire group. (See the collaborative lesson on globalization or create one of your own.)
4. The leader/facilitator should read the assignment or students can take turns reading it.
5. The leader/facilitator should give everyone in the group an opportunity to respond.
6. If there is a question for the teacher, the group leader should be the one to ask it. Perhaps someone in the group already knows the answer.
7. It is best to start with short group activities that can be completed during one or two class periods for at least one card marking before making longer assignments. Each group member should keep a copy/record of whatever is done in the group.
8. Remind students to NOT TRUST ONE MEMBER to keep all of the materials and notes from any working session.

About Group Leaders
Group leaders/facilitators can be selected by the group, or they can volunteer, each month or each card marking. They can earn extra credit for serving as the leader. Group members determine whether the leader has done an excellent job, a good job, a fair job, or a poor job.

Dear Student,
"Partners pool knowledge and understanding of everything from spelling to life experiences. Partners raise morale, spread responsibility, share and balance emotions, and provide social satisfaction."

—James Moffett,
Active Voice

The classroom is a social, moral, and academic community. It is community forged out of fair play, struggle, laughter, arguments, fun, respect, anger, and trust. It is a supportive environment that allows you to grow intellectually and emotionally. We will work with and for one another. In the world of work, people must learn to compete, to work autonomously, as well as to work as part of a team. Often employees lose jobs not because of talent, but because they cannot get along. A global economy requires becoming skilled in working with others to achieve goals. A "flat world" requires developing the capacity to perform civilly in more than one cultural setting.

You will be divided into groups of four or five. I will circulate from group to group to monitor and provide support.

Face-to-Face seating serves to:
1. Afford you opportunities to think through and discuss ideas, information, and problems under peer and teacher guidance.
2. Afford everyone the opportunity to participate in discussion, not just the same five or six students.
3. Furnish a small, authentic audience for reading and writing assignments where you can learn to reflect on and to evaluate your own ideas, and those of others.
4. Create a situation that gives experiences in leading and in following.
5. Provide a support group. Your confidence as an individual can be enhanced through success in a group.
6. Provide an opportunity to work effectively in a civil manner with individuals who have different expertise and/or who come from different cultural backgrounds.

Rules for Getting Started
1. Enter the room with a cooperative spirit. In life, our attitude will determine our altitude.
2. Listen attentively to what the other group members are saying. Respect differing ideas and opinions. Remember, we criticize ideas and not people.
3. The manner of speaking is as important as the matter. Our feelings should be expressed in a positive manner.
4. Each group member must learn to verbalize his/her point of view.
5. If a question calls for an opinion and you do not agree with a group member, do NOT change your mind unless you are logically persuaded. Be strong; it is acceptable to defend a belief.

Selecting a Group Leader/Facilitator/Spokesperson

"Snowflakes are nature's most fragile objects, but look what they accomplish when they stick together".

Vesta Kelly, Educator

The group leader is a guide or a conductor. S/he is a facilitator, making life easier for the group. If an individual has a question, s/he should ask group members instead of the teacher. The group leade/spokesperson raises his/her hand to pose the question to the teacher ONLY if no one in the group can explain the answer.

A Group Leader:
1. Has good attendance.
2. Keeps ALL group members on task.
3. Is in charge of distributing and collecting books/materials.
4. Asks questions/probes; helps to build consensus when necessary.
5. Keeps the peace.
6. Other (Explain)

The group leader will earn extra credit for taking on this responsibility.

Guiding Principle 2.2

Teachers are aware that community is people with whom we share our stories, promoting a sense of belonging. Teachers engage students "bonding" or "getting to know you" activities.

Student Sheet
Inner Assets, Liabilities, Traits, and Roles,

These words describe you and the people you read about, see on TV, in movies and in real life. Which assets will advance your career opportunities in a 21st century, innovation-based global economy? Which terms are positive, negative or neutral? Why? Which ones refer to you? Share them with your group members.

Keep these terms in your folder.

ambitious	dainty	perseverant	tenacious
anxious	foolish	serious	talented 10th
arrogant	efficient	sensitive	triumphant
articulate	disagreeable	social elite	vitality
authoritarian	dedicated	rowdy	serious
bashful	disrespectful	optimistic	snob
blunt	delicate	pathetic	self-disciplined
boisterous	entrepreneur	superficial	scholarly
	fame		truth
bully	humorous	pitiful	tyrant
captain	idealist	outgoing	titan
chameleon	miserly	honest	
chameleon	eccentric	sentimental	sentimental
charismatic	faddist	shy	unprincipled
civilized	feeble-minded	greed	winner
confident	loyal	president	peace
content	gallant	philosophical	
controlled	hot-tempered	steadfast	leader
courageous	irresponsible	shallow	optimistic
critical	leader	principled	boastful
curious	jealous	persuasive	status
glory	glory	power	
decisive	kingpin	opportunist	
determined	bellicose	sociable	wealth
director	grateful	open-minded	governor
egotistical	gullible	peaceful	presidential
energetic	naive	obstinate	Ceo
envious	misfit	prevaricator	maverick
even-tempered	mayoral	resolute	renegade

Who Are You - Really?

We can gain insight to people in a variety of ways: how they behave, what others say, what they say about themselves.

Are you one person in front of your family, friends, classmates, but someone else online? Do you assume a different personal (role) in a chat room where you can present yourself as being an age, gender, or personality of your own choosing: flashy and outgoing instead of quiet and thoughtful? WHO ARE YOU, REALLY?

Complete the graphic organizer about you. When you have finished the task, you will share it with others in your group.

You may use the Inner Assets, Traits, and Roles chart to complete your response.

What are your dominant traits and values? Give proof.

How do you generally behave or act? Give an example.

What are your inner thoughts and feelings? Give proof.

What are your values and beliefs? Give an example.

What do others say about you? Give proof.

Group Processing Skills—Affective Domain

Dr. Benjamin Bloom focused most of his career on the study of educational objectives and proposed that any task stimulates one of the three psychological domains: cognitive, affective, or psychomotor. Most academic classrooms engage primarily in the cognitive and affective domains. The cognitive domain deals with knowledge and understanding of concepts or ideas. The affective domain is concerned with the attitudes, feelings, and motivations that result from the learning process.

Students need a vocabulary to assess the social/affective realm. Students should keep these terms in their notebooks/folders and use them systematically to provide constructive feedback on where they are in the collaborative process. Keep in mind that a community is forged out of struggle, fun, arguments, joy, tears, and anger; therefore, conflict will occur.

Bloom's Affective Domain Vocabulary		
acclaims	cooperates	joins
agrees	defends	offers
argues	disagrees	participates in
assumes	disputes	praises
attempts	engages in	resists
avoids	helps	shares
challenges	is attentive to	volunteers

Reflecting on How Well the Group/Team Is Doing
My family/team members share…
The group leader challenges…
As a team/group we avoid….
I seem to resist…

Face-to-Face: Fostering Individual Accountability and Interdependence

Collaborative Learning Lesson: Globalization

Goal: *To practice and reinforce interdependence and individual accountability through an assignment that examines the principles of a global workforce.*

Follow the Leader *(Individual Activity)*

We have all had experiences in leading and following. Recall a time when you were in charge. Write the entry in your journal or blog, but be prepared to share it with your group members.

1. *Where were you?*
2. *Who was expected to follow your lead?*
3. *What were you in charge of?*
4. *Why were you in charge (took charge, given the charge, worked your way up)?*
5. *How did it turn out? What were your FEELINGS and THOUGHTS about leadership? Use some of the terms from the traits and roles chart.*

The World Is Flat Assignment

It is the year 2020. You are the president of a global company employing 100 persons in five major cities throughout the world. Your offices are virtual, meaning that your employees work from home or their automobile and connect to you and to one another via a computer. You never "see" one another except through video software, and you communicate primarily through e-mail, company website, social networks.

You need five new employees to replace the ones you had to fire because they could not succeed in this environment. You must create a new job description to post on your website.

Interdependence: Discuss with your group the requirements for such a job. What are the skills, traits, values needed to succeed in this global environment?

Share with the entire class.

The group leader can create a gallery walk chart to document the group's views. Everyone in the class will have access to these charts, which can be especially helpful for students who are absent when this activity is done.

Independent/ Individual Accountability:

Write 150 words or less:

- Give your company a name and a rationale for its existence. What is your URL?
- Write a job description for this position; provide a job title.

Assessment:

- ❑ Thesis statement (umbrella statement)
- ❑ Unity (sticks to the topic)
- ❑ Coherence (organization)
- ❑ Language choices
- ❑ Insight
- ❑ Syntax (sentence structure)
- ❑ Grammar and mechanics

Core Area:
Highly Effective Teachers
Create Systems
3.0

Building a safe, orderly community requires dedication, energy, managing time, setting priorities, delegating tasks. If there is no system or routine, every day is different, creating chaos.

Highly Effective Teachers Create Systems: Rituals and Routines

Journey Stop 3.0

"Most people surveying the world around them today see only chaos. They suffer a sense of personal powerlessness and pointlessness. Individuals need life structure. The absence of structure breeds breakdown."

Alvin Toffler, *The Third Wave*

Highly effective teachers establish a classroom community with clearly defined systems, including rituals, routines, and polices, that leave a positive, emotional imprint/impression/mark on students. Students keep and replay in memory the daily rhythms and routines of the classroom, which explains why students thrive in some classrooms and flounder in others. They are recapturing a positive or negative experience.

System	an orderly way of getting things done; organization, not random or by chance; a set of things or parts forming a whole
Routine	doing the same things in the same way disciplined in habit, practice, and procedure
Ritual	a series of steps undertaken prior to the execution of a task; in time, routines can become ritual and create memories, like a ceremony
Policy	a plan of action; a way of governing

Rather than reacting on the spot to challenges or events, which can contribute to the development of undesirable behaviors, systems invite the teacher to address and plan for the most stubborn problems of everyday classroom life. By eliminating the fear of the unknown, established rituals, routines, and policies provide the psychological and emotional safety crucial to taking intellectual risks (Abraham Maslow). Highly effective teachers promote a clean, safe, orderly, AND predictable classroom community. Systems communicate to students that while there may be chaos in the world, there is none in the classroom.

Added Conversation: Integrate your experience and expertise to share with the teacher. You might want to share this activity with your face-to-face team or with a social networking professional learning community.

Notes

"We don't receive wisdom; we must discover it for ourselves after a journey that no one can take for us or spare us." Marcel Proust

Owl Mountain Principles

Dear Teacher, Do You Create Systems: Rituals and Routines?

Reflect on the principles listed below. What principles can you teach or share with others (assets)? What are your areas for growth: undeveloped or underdeveloped? In the blank space, write a conversation/comment to share with a coach/teacher leader other trusted professional. What goals do you need to set?

CONVERSATIONS WITH A COACH

Assets   Underdeveloped Assets   Undeveloped Assets

3.1   I have developed a syllabus that outlines the framework for success from August/September through June/July.

3.2   I have rituals/routines in place that make good use of time at the beginning of the period, the end (closure) of the period, and preclude loss of instructional time.

3.3   I require and MONITOR that students bring a notebook and folder to class EACH day because they are crucial to the learning process.

3.4   I give comprehensive midterm assessments and comprehensive final assessments because learning is cumulative (state-mandated tests are based on comprehensive knowledge and skills).

3.5   My system for assessment (grading) is rarely challenged by students, parents, or the office because it is public, consistent, and ongoing. My students can compute their grades on their own.

3.6   I have a discipline approach/plan in place that is firm, fair, and consistent. I seldom send students to the office.

Journal/Create a vision statement for creating systems (rituals and routines). Describe your "inner assets."

Conversations for the Journey

Dear Coach,

As you navigate *The Journey from Compliance to Community* with teachers, the sample "conversations" on the next pages will help you find your voice during the tough spots.

Modify or edit what I have written to suit your situation. Integrate YOUR insights about how highly effective teachers: create systems. These "conversations" will build your schema. Think of them as a starting point. Exchange "conversations" with your professional learning community.

Lorraine Richardson, Chief Owl

P.S. How do you know which teachers have created systems? How can you pair them with other teachers?

Creating Systems: Rituals and Routines

Principle 3.0

If there are no systems or routines, every day is different, creating chaos. Without routines, there is nothing to improve upon. Systems allow you to spend more time interfacing with students and to conserve energy. Does the classroom promote a clean, safe, and orderly environment, an environment where students feel secure and protected enough to learn? (Abraham Maslow)

Think about why establishments such as Starbucks, Kinko's, Federal Express, and The Holiday Inn are so successful. Their customers know what the *experience* will be every time. A SYSTEM is in place that leverages ordinary employees to produce extraordinary results over and over (Michael Gerber, *The E-Myth Revisited*).

Systems build a consistency to the learning experience.

Guiding Principle 3.1   Teachers have developed a syllabus that outlines the framework for success from August/September through June/July **(school culture).**

The syllabus is the blueprint, the guide, the fundamental principles, the structure, and the vision of the classroom. Making clear the demands of time and energy, the syllabus provides the opportunity to share with students and parents our plan and to get them to commit to it. A syllabus lets them know that we are going to be together for the next ten to twelve months, therefore, it is important that we learn and understand the framework for success. The syllabus is the opportunity to reinforce credibility by anticipating all of the challenges to be faced throughout the school year and to plan for them.

Added Comments/Conversations: Integrate your experience and expertise.

Guiding Principle 3.2   Teachers have rituals/routines in place that make good use of time at the beginning of the period, the end (closure) of the period, precluding a loss of instructional time.

The opportunity to learn is nothing short of staggering if you subtract holidays, field trips, and outings, end-of-the-year activities, half-days, and PA announcements. Couple these interruptions with a loss of ten minutes a day (through classroom mismanagement) and students lose months and years of instructional time.

Losing ten minutes daily multiplied by five days a week equals the loss of ONE fifty-minute instructional period. This fifty minutes multiplied by forty weeks amounts to two months of instructional time lost. It is as if students meet from September through April instead of from September through June. Multiply this TEN-minute DAILY loss by four years and students have lost ONE WHOLE YEAR of instructional time.

Added Comments/Conversations: Integrate your experience and expertise.

Guiding Principle 3.3   Teachers require and MONITOR that students bring a notebook and folder to class EACH day because they aid memory and the continuity of the learning process **(school culture).**

Notebooks/academic logs are the reservoir of knowledge that demonstrates the serious intellectual act of learning. As an ongoing record of what transpires in class, they should be the equivalent of an ID card and a necessity to enter the classroom, especially for high school students. Containing summaries, explanations of concepts, examples of algorithms, and class notes, academic logs (one for EACH class) serve as concrete examples of what students are learning in class each day and are the BEST exemplars of "student work." Writing is brain-based learning that supports encoding.

The maintenance of notebooks and folders (with old assignments and tests) allows parents to participate in the process. Though in some schools, students keep online (virtual) notebooks, that process EXCLUDES many parents (especially low-income) from being involved in the day-to-day happenings of the classroom because all work is behind a user ID and password. However, physical academic logs empower parents through easy access to open and question the child about what's going on in school.

An effective method for a disciplinary conference with a student and/or parent is to begin with the notebooks—no notebooks, nothing learned. No need to discuss behavior, student complaints, or parent complaints because the so- called "student" is really a trespasser and should be treated accordingly.

There can be NO sustained adequate yearly progress (AYP) improvement without notebooks AND folders. Learning requires the continuity required by a notebook. Distributing color-coded folders (blue for math, green for science, etc.) further aids in the organization of students.

Added Comments/Conversations: Integrate your experience and expertise.

Guiding Principle 3.4   Teachers give *comprehensive* midterm assessments and comprehensive final assessments because learning is cumulative (state-mandated tests are based on comprehensive knowledge and skills) **[school culture].**

Too often, the mid-term or final exam becomes whatever students studied last: the last chapters, the last novel, the last algorithms, the last concepts. Sometimes this occurs because the school culture does not support comprehensive mid-terms or comprehensive final exams. It's easier for teachers to prepare a test on the most recently covered material and count it as a double grade than it is to go back and select critical information from the beginning of the term. However, most textbooks include chapter tests, unit tests, and summary tests which should be administered. Notebooks/academic logs assist in the comprehensive assessment process because they can be used to review all work learned. State-mandated tests and national exams such as the ACT or SAT are tests of students' TOTAL learning experiences.

Added Comments/Conversations: Integrate your experience and expertise. What opposition do you anticipate teachers will provide for not administering comprehensive exams?

Guiding Principle 3.5   A teacher's system for assessment (grading) is rarely challenged by students, parents, or the office because it is public, consistent, and ongoing. Students understand their strength/improvement areas and can compute their grades on their own.

Keeping an up-to-date grade book (hard copy or online) and a transparent grading system reduce conflict. Grades can breed a sense of powerlessness because grades equal self-worth to many students. Grades improperly structured teach passivity (trait needed to succeed during the industrial era) rather than democracy. Students must submit to authority because the locus of control is with the teacher and not with the student. This is especially true if they are used by the teacher to exert power or as a weapon. Because grades can create an avalanche of hostility, they are not appropriate tools for effective classroom management. Although there is NO foolproof method, true assessment should be a two-way process that is carried out through interaction between the teacher and the learner.

Assessments that are public and ongoing quantify students' strengths, weaknesses, and gaps, which give them a framework for validation and/or improvement. When they don't, they become a source of conflict, and the learning community breaks down as grades are challenged by students, parents, and/or administrators. Be certain to communicate the criteria for success in advance for ALL assignments. The assessment/grading policy should be outlined in the syllabus.

Added Comments/Conversations: Integrate your experience and expertise. How can you support teachers with high failure rates? Who are the leading thinkers on assessment practices?

Guiding Principle 3.6   Teachers have a discipline approach/plan in place that is firm, fair, and consistent. They seldom send students to the office.

A behavior system needs to be in place that creates community instead of compliance. Because we are no longer preparing students for the factory or the repetitive tasks of an office (Secondary teachers, take note!), a classroom community must be created that promotes an environment in which troublesome behavior is solved together.

What are the patterns of behavior in your classroom? Which behaviors are NORMAL DEVELOPMENT (they come with the job) versus those that are DEVIANT (require outside intervention)? List the top five behaviors that predominate in the classroom. Can you identify the students who are the primary violators of the behaviors? Who owns the behavior problems (students, teachers, school, community, society, parents)? Is the classroom a hostile learning environment? If so, which behaviors cause it to be so? How do you enlist students to develop a community in which troublesome behavior is solved together?

An effective teacher is firm, fair, consistent, and persistent because s/he knows that a lack of order breeds disorder and invites frustration. Because today too many students' lives are often a perpetual storm of emotional and spiritual distress, the classroom community needs to be an emotionally safe and orderly environment.

Though there is NO foolproof system, whatever it is should be described in the syllabus for parents and students. The principles of the system should be practiced often until they are internalized by students. It is up to much debate about the best approach for classroom management. Ultimately it is up to you and/or the school to choose which approach will work best to improve student behavior and create a classroom community that operates as an efficient learning environment.

Some leading thinkers on this topic are John Dewey, Alfie Kohn, Abraham Maslow, B.F. Skinner, Lee Canter, and William Glasser.

Added Comments/Conversations: Integrate your experience and expertise. Does the school or district promote a particular discipline system?

Asset Building Activities 3.0

Creating Systems: Rituals and Routines

- **3.1   The Syllabus**
- **3.2   Instructional Time Management**
- **3.3   The Academic Log/Notebook**
- **3.5   Clean, Emotionally Safe, and Orderly**

The Owl Mountain Coaching ™ Asset Building activities on the following pages are aligned with the core area, creating systems. Each activity is a standalone module containing principles that effective teachers practice intuitively at an unconscious level, much like an outstanding athlete who is "in the zone," executing plays without being able to explain why or how. With your patience and staying power, these activities will encourage in-depth exchange about teacher quality and classroom practices.

We are what we repeatedly do; excellence then is not an act, but a habit.

Aristotle

A Syllabus = the Constitution, the Vision, the Blueprint

Creating Systems
Guiding Principle 3.1: I have developed a syllabus that outlines the framework for success from August through June and beyond.

Goals: The coach will work with teachers to:
- Create a vision of the classroom as a *community* of learners.
- Understand the importance of a syllabus in reinforcing their credibility.
- Develop a syllabus that supports and reinforces the curriculum, instruction, and assessment/grading practices of the school, school district, and/or the state.

Time Allotment:
60 to 90 minutes to begin the process
The syllabus can be completed during a series of departmental (content area) meetings, or through social networking: live chats, discussion boards, wikis.

Materials:
Template for developing a syllabus
Model syllabus included or syllabi from highly effective teachers
State standards
School district curriculum framework
School discipline policy
School assessment/grading practices policy
Giant Post-its or flipchart for outlining

How will you select the audience for this activity?
- ✓ New teachers?
- ✓ Self-selection? Nomination?
- ✓ Whole staff?
- ✓ Parents

Coaching Support:
What relationships or alliances do you need to build in order to make this activity successful? Highly effective teachers who exhibit an exemplary teaching voice and the accompanying body language? Leadership team? A virtual professional learning community (VPLC)?

Maintenance:
Because this is a formative assessment activity, what kind of follow-up will be necessary?

Instructions:

Encourage teachers to sit in groups of four, or by content area, or by grade level. Select one of the two opening activities:

Opening activity 1: Ask teachers to close their eyes and dream about their classrooms.

CONVERSATIONS WITH A COACH

- What do they feel, hear, and see going on?
- How does the class begin, and how does it end?
- What kind of teaching and learning activities are taking place?
- What role, if any, does technology play?
- How are students behaving? What is the culture of the classroom?
- What is the teacher's role?

Ask teachers to share their vision of their classrooms with their group. Create a master chart. Or you may want to create an online environment for this activity.

Opening activity 2: Ask teachers to write a one-page vision statement about their classrooms that include the components previously listed. Encourage teachers to share their visions: face-to-face or online.

Read/share the information about the purpose of the syllabus.

Distribute the template and encourage teachers to begin filling in as much as possible. Distribute the model syllabus provided or additional models from high-performing teachers. This is an appropriate time for teachers to sit and work by content areas if they did not during the opening activity.

Syllabus Background Information

The syllabus is the blueprint, the guide, the fundamental principles, the structure, and the vision of our classroom. It serves the same purpose as our CONSTITUTION.

When the founding fathers developed our Constitution, they were aware that they were developing a document that would have to last for ages and yet kept in mind what the ages would produce, according to James Madison, a founding father.

The syllabus becomes a document that must last from August through June and beyond. As it is developed, keep in mind what must be established and kept in place for the entire school year. This is the opportunity to share with students and parents the learning plan and to get them to commit to it. To let them know that we are going to be together for the next 200 days or more, it is important that we learn and understand the framework for success. All challenges must be thought through. This is the chance to **reinforce our credibility**.

Instead of starting with too much content too soon at the beginning of the school year, we need to invest in the guidelines and principles in our syllabus. Often we go over the syllabus one or two times and then we put it away, thinking that students remember what we've said, but they don't. They have four or more other teachers who have developed and read a syllabus to them. We must give them an opportunity to practice and to reinforce the contents in order that they remember. Whenever there is a breakdown in the classroom community, it is helpful to revisit the syllabus orally with students. It keeps them focused on the *"Why We Are Here,"* on the thousands of taxpayer dollars being spent on their education, on the clear expectations, and on the vision. Students should keep a copy in their folder.

Added Comments/Conversations: Integrate your experience and expertise.

"In framing a system which we wish to last for the ages, we should not lose sight of the changes which the ages will produce." James Madison

Developing A Course Syllabus—A Template

Working in groups by content area, begin completing the template. Identify the areas where you want to build uniformity. A common language supports consistent, predictable results and creates a positive school culture. You might want to create a live chat, a forum, or a wiki to support this activity.

Course Description

Describe the course in a paragraph and outline the important goals. Read the state standards and/or the school district curriculum.

Textbook/Supplementary Materials/Supplies

Will students be able to take the textbooks home? Will online textbooks play a role? What is the role of technology in your classroom and with the curriculum? How often will students need to use a computer to complete assignments?

Vision/Structure

The classroom is the canvas on which learning is painted.
Students come to us at-risk and the environment we create or fail to create further puts them at risk. How do you see students learning and interacting? What kind of culture do you want to create in your classroom: collaborative learning, project-based centers, peer response groups, literature circles, etc.? How much learning will take place outside of the classroom?

Classroom Rules AND Consequences

Rules are for the minority who will break them".

What are the rituals, routines, and systems necessary for success in the community? We need to think out rules carefully so that every consequence is not developed on the spot. Not communicating and reinforcing clear expectations leads to inconsistency and irrational decisions, which undermine us as teachers. Does your school or district support a particular classroom management philosophy?

Homework Policy

Homework levels should be consistent. Students should not have projects, tests, or reports assigned at the last minute. Give students a timeline so that they can plan. Homework should be used to review and reinforce information introduced in class. It is NOT a time for new concepts.

Make-Up Policy

Whatever the policy is, it should be consistent. Consistency keeps from having to give out busy work just before the end of a report card marking.

System of Assessment/Grading

Report card grades should not be a surprise. Assessment should be clear, consistent, public, and ongoing. Students who are lacking intrinsic motivation need daily/weekly reminders of their progress or lack of progress. Grades should be composed of a variety of activities and assignments. Students should be able to compute their own grades. Grades are NOT an effective classroom management tool/weapon. The teacher should NOT be the sole arbiter of excellence.

Course Syllabus for English 2A   **Instructor L. Richardson**

Sample Syllabus

Martin Luther King, Jr. Senior High School
3000 East Lafayette
Detroit, Michigan 48207

Course Description

The ninth-grade course introduces students to high school English and is designed to lay a foundation for future success. Three major components of English (literature, composition, and oral language) are presented with a view to assisting students in their basic and cultural literary growth. There is a heavy emphasis on writing, and writing assignments stem from literary selections. Writing is process-based, and guides students from the simple paragraph through the more complex five-part paper. Students will be introduced to essential research skills, including using search engines, constructing a bibliography and formulating a thesis statement. Grammar instruction is presented not as a series of isolated drills, but rather as an integral part of oral and written communication.

Writing Goals/Objectives

Students will:
1. Recognize that writing is a way to learn and develop.
2. Use pre-writing activities to generate ideas, deepen concepts, develop logical thinking, record observations, and extend vocabulary.
3. Express themselves in writing for a variety of purposes and authentic audiences.
4. Revise their composition to sharpen their ideas and to improve organization, tone, and style.
5. Proofread their writing to correct punctuation, spelling, grammar, and form.
6. Publish their writing in order to share it with an authentic audience.

Reading Goals/Objectives:

Students will:
1. Construct meaning.
2. Develop positive attitudes and perceptions about reading.
3. Obtain knowledge about the text genre and structures that occur in required reading.
4. Learn about tasks that require responses or follow-up reading.
5. Use strategies necessary to process text: print literacy vs. online literacy.
6. Acquire necessary background knowledge and context needed to process content.

7. Practice cognitive skills required to construct meaning from text and online mediums.

Basic Text and Supplementary Materials/Supplies
Voices in a Tradition
Farenheit 451
Of Mice and Men
To Kill a Mockingbird
I Know Why the Caged Bird Sings
Unabridged or collegiate dictionary for home use, or an online reference, if available
Thesaurus for home use, or an online version, if available
Spiral notebook, blue or black ink pen, Post-it notes

Basic Class Structure/Vision—The Collaborative Learning Community

The classroom is a social, moral, and academic community. It is community forged out of fair play, struggle, laughter, arguments, fun, respect, anger, and trust. It is a supportive environment that allows you to grow intellectually and emotionally. We will work with and for one another. In the world of work, people must learn to compete, to work autonomously, as well as to work as part of a team. Often employees lose jobs not because of talent, but because they cannot get along. A global economy requires becoming skilled in working with others to achieve goals. A "flat world" requires developing the capacity to perform civilly in more than one cultural setting.

You will be divided into groups of four or five. I will circulate from group to group to monitor and provide support.

The Collaborative Community serves to:
1. Afford you opportunities to think through and discuss ideas, information, and problems under peer and teacher guidance.
2. Afford everyone the opportunity to participate in discussion, not just the same five or six students.
3. Furnish a small, authentic audience for reading and writing assignments where you can learn to reflect on and to evaluate your own ideas, and those of others.
4. Create a situation that gives experiences in leading and in following.
5. Provide a support group. Your confidence as an individual can be enhanced through success in a group.
6. Provide an opportunity to work effectively in a civil manner with individuals who have different expertise and/or who come from different cultural backgrounds.

Rules for Getting Started

1. Enter the room with a cooperative spirit. In life, our attitude will determine our altitude.
2. Listen attentively to what the other group members are saying. Respect differing ideas and opinions. Remember, we criticize ideas and not people.

3. The manner of speaking is as important as the matter. Our feelings should be expressed in a positive manner.
4. Each group member must learn to verbalize his/her point of view.
5. If a question calls for an opinion and you do not agree with a group member, do NOT change your mind unless you are logically persuaded. Be strong; it is acceptable to defend a belief.

Selecting a Group Leader/Facilitator/Spokesperson

The group leader is a guide or a conductor. S/he is a facilitator, making life easier for the group. If an individual has a question, s/he should ask group members instead of the teacher. The group leader raises his/her hand to pose the question to the teacher ONLY if no one in the group can explain the answer.

A Group Leader:
1. Has good attendance.
2. Keeps ALL group members on task.
3. Is in charge of distributing and collecting books/materials.
4. Asks questions/probes; helps to build consensus when necessary.
5. Keeps the peace.

The group leader will earn extra credit for taking on this responsibility.

Classroom Rules and Consequences
Because attendance, preparation, and effort are crucial to the objectives of the course, we will start each card marking with a bank of 300 credits/points.

1. Each ***unexcused*** absence will result in five credits being subtracted. You must bring a note from home or a school employee to excuse the absence ***within seventy-two (72) hours*** of your return to class or the absence WILL NOT be excused. The teacher will keep a file of all excuses.
2. Every second unexcused tardiness will result in five credits being subtracted. A tardy excuse must be signed by a school employee who IS NOT a relative.
3. Each time you are ***unprepared*** for class, five credits will be subtracted. In order to be **prepared** for class, you will need **ALL** of the following:
   ❑ A COOPERATIVE SPIRIT
   ❑ Blue or black ink pen or a number 2 pencil (Nothing else is acceptable.)
   ❑ Textbook
   ❑ Spiral notebook with at least 100 pages (not to be used as loose-leaf paper)
   ❑ Loose-leaf paper

❑ Folder with all assignments, past and present.
❑ Appropriate Dress (School Dress Code)

4. All work is to be turned in on time. All work must be completed and directions followed. Once an assignment has been corrected and returned to the class, that particular assignment CANNOT be turned in for credit.

5. No **personal** cell phones, MP3 players, CDs/DVDs, etc. will be tolerated. If these instruments are needed, the school will provide them or specific instructions/timelines will be provided for their use. If a personal instrument is in view for ANY reason, it will be taken and given to an administrator. A conference will be scheduled with a parent.

Homework Policy

In order to perform well on pop quizzes, announced tests, written work, and oral assignments, time must be spent at home in preparation. You should spend approximately thirty to fifty minutes, five evenings a week, practicing and reviewing information covered in class. If you follow the timeline, you won't be caught off-guard.

Make-Up Policy

Being absent from class places an unusually heavy burden on you to learn information without the benefit of the discussion, visual aids, diagrams, and examples, that accompany a lesson. When you are absent, you miss an experience that can never be recreated. Nevertheless, absence from class is no excuse for not completing classroom requirements. ***All assignments must be made up within seventy-two (72) hours of your return to class after an EXCUSED absence.*** *It is YOUR RESPONSIBILTIY to find out what was missed to make up the work.*

Extra credit work WILL NOT be given to make up for assignments missed. Extra credit/enrichment assignments are given to students who are working at a level of excellence and who want/need more of a challenge. However, the opportunity to earn extra credit points will be INTEGRATED into regularly assigned work and tests.

Assessment/Grades

We will use a point system to compute grades. Each card marking, we will complete ***approximately*** 1,000-1,200 credits of work (includes 300 points for participation, attendance, and effort). Because learning is cumulative, you will take a comprehensive mid-term and final exam. Once each semester, you will complete a Web quest or social networking activity in place of a traditional writing assignment. You will be given a calendar on which to keep a running tally of your credits.

Participation, Attendance, and Effort	300 Credits
Notebook	200 Credits
Oral Participation	100 Credits
Tests, Quizzes	300 Credits **(Approximately)**
Compositions, Blogs, Essays, Short-Answer Assignments	<u>300 Credits</u> **(Approximately)**
TOTAL	1,200 Credits/Points

90 – 100% = A   80 – 89% = B   70 – 79% = C   60 – 69% = D

0 – 59 % = FAILURE

"Luck is a crossroads where preparation and opportunity meet."

We all have the same twenty-four hours in a day; it is what makes us equal. What we do with them is what makes us different.

Instructional Time Management:
Adding Weeks and Months to the School Calendar

Creating Systems

Guiding Principle 3.2: I have systems (rituals/routines/procedures) in place that make good use of time at the beginning of the period and at the end of the period, precluding a loss of instructional time and increasing the opportunity to learn.

Goals:
The teacher leader will help teachers:

- Audit their time management in the classroom.
- Share strategies for managing time productively in the learning community.
- Create a plan for adding weeks and/or months to the school calendar through instructional time management.

Time Allotment: 60 to 90 minutes

Materials:
Twelve-question quiz
Answer key
Time Management Quiz scoring guide

Who is the audience for this activity?
- ✓ Staff meetings
- ✓ Content or grade-level meetings
- ✓ One-on-one teacher support
- ✓ Whole faculty
- ✓ New teachers, marginal teachers

Support: What relationships or alliances do you need to build in order to make this activity successful? Highly effective teachers? Leadership team? A virtual professional learning network.

Maintenance:
Because this is a formative assessment activity, what follow-up is necessary?

Instructions:

Review the "conversation" that accompanies guiding principle 3.2.

Encourage teachers to sit in pairs or in groups of four, honoring an equal voice and an equal regard. Would you like to create an online network for this activity?

- ✓ Ask teachers for examples of how they and students lose time each day in the classroom, which keeps them from achieving their instructional goals.
- ✓ Ask teachers about time-saving strategies they use to achieve instructional goals more efficiently.
- ✓ Distribute the quiz to teachers. Give them ten minutes to complete it.
- ✓ Go over the responses with them, indicating the point values for each item. Request that teachers keep track of their points.
- ✓ Distribute the Time Management Scoring Guide in order that teachers can determine if they are a highly effective teacher, a "needs improvement" teacher, or a time-thief teacher.
- ✓ Discuss the responses by addressing the underlying theory, best practices, and/or research for each question. Ask teachers for their input.
- ✓ Give teachers an opportunity to develop a plan to improve their time management in the classroom.

Conversations/Background

We all have the same 1,440 minutes in a day; it's what makes us the equal. What we do with them is what makes us different.

Time management is self-management. Often the reason less effective teachers give for not wanting to manage time is that it takes away from freedom and spontaneity. However, losing ten minutes per day of instructional time equals a weekly loss of fifty minutes or one instructional fifty-minute period. Multiplied by a forty-week school year, this time loss amounts to forty hours—almost two months of instructional time. Much research suggests that time on task is one of the single most crucial factors contributing to student achievement

Highly effective teachers have systems in place to help prevent time loss—allowing more time on task. Master teachers are aware of what they expect and need from students every minute of the instructional period.

Teachers may indicate that they lose time because of students' poor behavior, but as they take the quiz and review the responses, they might realize a lack of procedures and policies are a root cause of student misconduct.

The questions developed for the quiz are based on a global composite of time wasters from my years of working with teachers.

Added Experience/Expertise:

Time Management Quiz
Adding Weeks, Months, and Years to the School Calendar by Saving Ten Minutes Daily

	Complete this instructional time management quiz to determine if time in the community is managed productively.
1	Students can get started as soon as the bell rings/period starts without having to wait for me. A. Always B. Sometimes C. Hardly Ever
2	Students are required to keep a notebook in class with daily summaries on what we have learned. A. Always B. Sometimes C. Hardly Ever
3	I take attendance by calling everyone's name each day. A. Always B. Sometimes C. Hardly Ever
4	Students clean up five or ten minutes before the end of the period or are dismissed early. A. Always B. Sometimes C. Hardly Ever
5	I use a system that monitors class participation (discussion) in a manner that ensures equity and facilitates the pace of class discussion. A. Always B. Sometimes C. Hardly Ever
6	Bell work activities take up fifteen or more minutes of the period. A. Always B. Sometimes C. Hardly Ever

7.	I am aware of the amount of time I give students to complete a classroom activity. Activities are timed (kitchen timer, stop watch, digital timer, time on chalkboard) to monitor the duration students are given to begin and complete an activity. A. Always B. Sometimes C. Hardly Ever
8.	Folders, supplies, and/or other materials are distributed seamlessly and effortless by students. A. Always B. Sometimes C. Hardly Ever
9	Students engage in unmonitored seatwork (screenwork) activity (skill sheets, computer activities, chapter review questions, workbook activities). A. Always B. Sometimes C. Hardly Ever
10	Students use classroom time to look up the definitions of long word lists. A. Always B. Sometimes C. Hardly Ever
11	Students are given a timeline of assignments and activities by the month or card marking. A. Always B. Sometimes C. Hardly Ever
12	When cleaning up or during the minutes before the bell rings, I engage in "sponge activities" with my students. A. Always B. Sometimes C. Hardly Ever

Conversations about Principles and Practice of Time Management

Goal: To analyze the underlying research, theory, and/or best practice for the principles identified in
the quiz.

Ask teachers to calculate points based on the sample responses/conversations below. Incorporate your own "conversations" about instructional time management.

1.   Students can get started without me as soon as the bell rings.
        A = 5 points   B = 3 points   C = 1 point

Enough said! The instructional hour begins as soon as the bell rings. Students can be taught to start the learning process without the teacher. If the teacher is delayed for whatever reason, time is not wasted. There are activities that can be built into a daily routine without input from the teacher.

Added conversation: Integrate your experience and expertise.

2.   Students are required to keep a notebook in class with daily summaries on what was learned.

A = 15 points   B = 7 points   C = 1 point

Learning can be said to be a series of conceptually cohesive encounters over time. Notebooks facilitate learning continuity by serving as a reservoir of content knowledge. A daily account of what goes on in the class, the notebook can be used as a reference for students when they are absent. Instead of taking valuable instructional time to explain concepts learned, students can rely on one another for the information. They can then approach the teacher and state, "I would like the project sheet that was distributed in class when I was absent," or "I would like to make up the quiz that was given." When students communicate with the teacher, it should be to make a specific request.

Added conversation: Integrate your experience and expertise.

3.   I take attendance by calling everyone's name.

A = 1 point   B = 3 points   C = 5 points

        Teachers use calling attendance as a readiness activity, but it really is a waste of instructional time. A seating plan is more efficient. Again, there are learning activities that can be institutionalized that will build readiness (open your notebook, write today's date, and summarize what we learned in class yesterday).

Added conversation: Integrate your experience and expertise.

4. Students clean up five or ten minutes before the end of the period or are dismissed early.

A = 1 point   B = 5 points   C = 10 points

        Cleaning up early is a perfect way to lose one or two months of instructional time.

Added conversation: Integrate your experience and expertise

5. I use a system that monitors class participation (discussion) in a manner that ensures equity and facilitates the pace of class discussion.

A = 10 points   B = 5 points   C = 1 point

Discussion activities should move at a fairly quick pace to sustain interest and not waste time. Writing each student's name on two or three small index cards, shuffling the cards, and then calling on students at random ensures equity and increases time on task. Ask the question first and then call on the student (Madeline Hunter, *Mastery Teaching*). Make a decision; s/he does or does not receive credit, and move on.

Added conversation: Integrate your experience and expertise.

6. Bell work activities take up fifteen or more minutes of the period.

A = 1 point   B = 3 points   C = 5 points

Bell work serves as a review and readiness activity. It should not supplant the time needed for new learning that takes place in the classroom.

Added conversation: Integrate your experience and expertise.

7. I am aware of the amount of time I give students to complete a classroom activity. Activities are timed (kitchen timer, stop watch, digital timer, time on chalkboard) to monitor the duration students are given to begin and complete an activity.

A = 10 points   B = 5 points   C = 1 point

Timing and time limits are two ways of using time to manage student behavior. They involve giving students predetermined amounts of time to work on some assigned task/project: "I'm going to give you twenty minutes to complete this activity." By setting the timer or by noting the time on the board, we raise a student's level of concern (Madeline Hunter, *Mastery Teaching*). If students are struggling to complete the assignment, more time can be added. However, if they are wasting time, let the chips fall where they may.

Also, the ACT is a timed test. Making students aware of time limits on a regular basis will support their preparation for this assessment.

Added conversation: Integrate your experience and expertise.

8. Folders, supplies, and/or other materials are distributed seamlessly and effortless by students.

A = 5 points   B = 3 points   C = 1 point

Daily procedures for how and when materials, supplies, and folders are distributed reduce confusion and time off task. If students are expected to bring all of these items, then daily consequences for not bringing them should be in place.

Added conversation: Integrate your experience and expertise.

9. Students engage in unmonitored seatwork or screenwork activity (skill sheets, software activities, chapter review questions, workbook activities).

A = 15 points   B = 8 points   C = 1 point

Often lower-order thinking activities such as chapter reviews are assigned to keep students busy and to avoid discipline problems. The majority of instructional time should be spent on the critical thinking and problem-solving needed to be successful in a knowledge-based economy. Some research demonstrates that students are often off task during lengthy unmonitored seatwork. If it can be completed without monitoring, then it can be assigned as homework.

Added conversation: Integrate your experience and expertise.

10. Students use classroom time to look up the definitions of word lists.

A = 1 point   B = 5 points   C = 10 points

Dictionary activities are used as low-level seatwork to keep students busy and again to avoid discipline problems. If students are repeatedly given long lists of words for which there is no pattern or connectedness, instructional time is being wasted. Learning can be said to be a process of understanding and remembering. What plan is in place for students to remember the words, other than rote memorization (industrial-era curriculum)?

Added conversation: Integrate your experience and expertise.

11. Students are given a timeline of assignments and activities by the month or by the card marking.

A = 5 points   B = 3 points   C = 1 point

Giving students a timeline allows them the opportunity to see a part of the master plan and to buy into it. It also saves time for students who are absent and allows for everyone to plan ahead. If you have created an online presence, it's an excellent way for parents to keep up with what's going on.

Added conversation: Integrate your experience and expertise

12. When cleaning up or during the minutes before the bell rings, I engage in "sponge activities" with my studentA = 10 points   B = 6 points   C = 1 point

First of all, the bell is a signal for the teacher. It is NOT a signal for the students to leave the room without permission. As students are packing or cleaning up, or if the clocks are off, engage students in a "sponge activity" or oral review activity. Sponging is soaking up every minute of available time; it is an activity that does not require supplies or materials. It is a time for reviewing concepts previously covered in class.

SPONGE ACTIVITY:

- ✓ Mary, identify three examples of conflict.
- ✓ Jason, you have ten red balls. What is the probability you will pick out a black ball? Explain.
- ✓ Marla, identify two causes of the French Revolution.
- ✓ Karl, explain adaptation and how being able to adapt to the surroundings might save an animal's life.

Scoring the Time Management Quiz

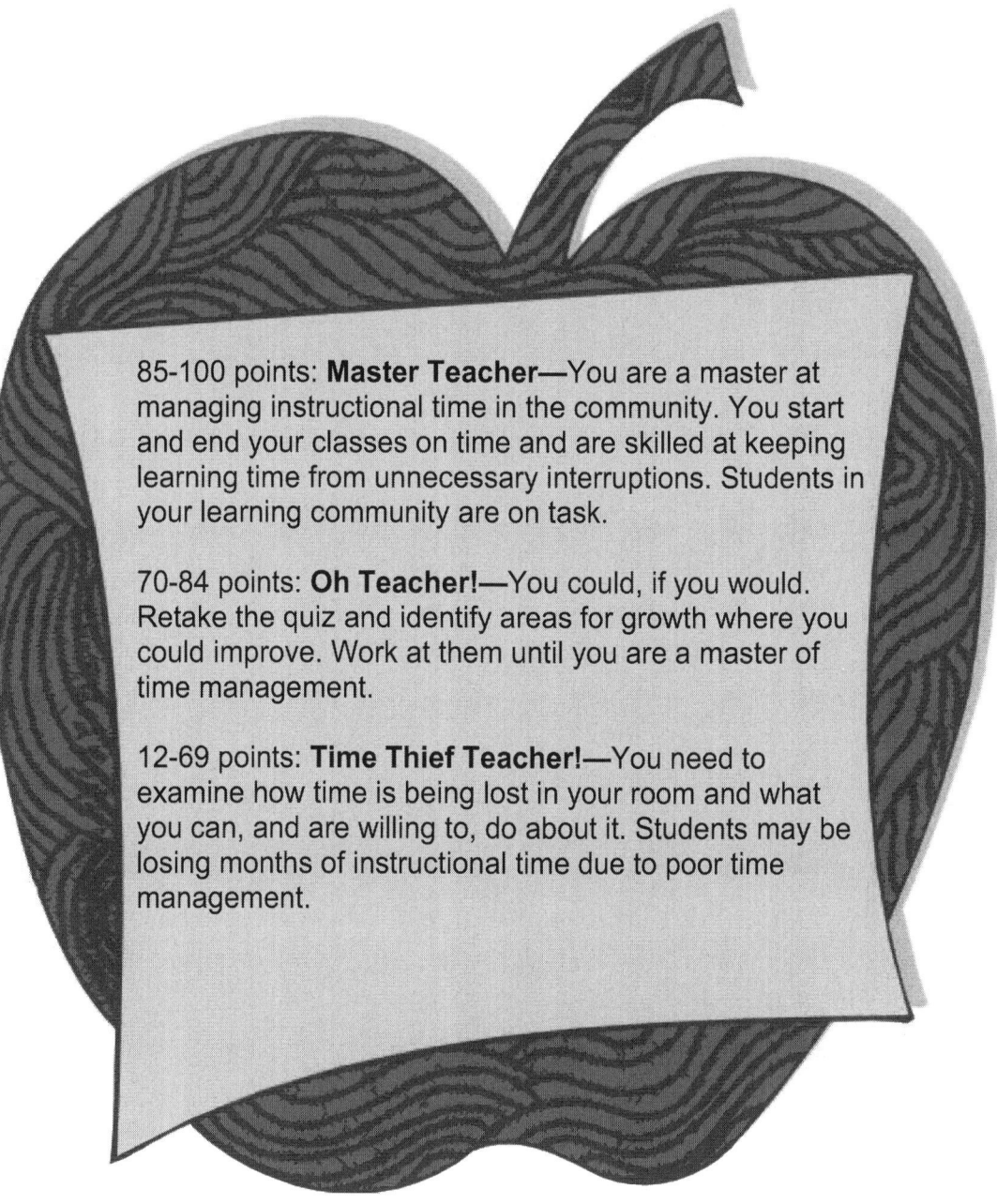

85-100 points: **Master Teacher**—You are a master at managing instructional time in the community. You start and end your classes on time and are skilled at keeping learning time from unnecessary interruptions. Students in your learning community are on task.

70-84 points: **Oh Teacher!**—You could, if you would. Retake the quiz and identify areas for growth where you could improve. Work at them until you are a master of time management.

12-69 points: **Time Thief Teacher!**—You need to examine how time is being lost in your room and what you can, and are willing to, do about it. Students may be losing months of instructional time due to poor time management.

Academic Log/Notebook as the Best Exemplar of Student Work

Creating Systems Guiding Principle 3.3

I require and MONITOR that students bring a notebook AND a folder to class EACH day because they are crucial to the learning process.

Goals
Teachers Will:
- Judge the notebook as the **best** exemplar of student work and understanding
- Appreciate how the notebook aids the learning and memory process.
- Investigate and establish the link between the notebook and success on tests.
- Understand how the notebook aids the reading and writing process in all content areas.
- Determine if there is a link between notebooks/folders and improving student achievement.
- Examine whether the culture of the school supports and reinforces students' maintaining a notebook and folder for EACH class. .
- Develop a school policy or system for implementation and monitoring of student notebooks and folders.
- Determine the role of parents in the policy.

Materials:
Each teacher should bring five to seven notebooks from their highest performing class and the same number from their lowest performing class. They should also bring the same number of folders from the same classes.

Who is the audience for this activity?
- ✓ Staff Meetings
- ✓ Content or Grade Level Meetings
- ✓ One-on-One Teacher Support,
- ✓ Professional Development Days – Whole Faculty
- ✓ Parent Meetings

Coaching Support
What relationships or alliances do you need to build in order to make this activity successful – highly effective teachers? Leadership team? A virtual professional network?

Maintenance
Because this is a formative assessment activity, what follow-up is necessary?

Instructions/Conversations
Encourage teachers to sit with their grade level or content area team.
Ask teachers to list the reasons students should keep notebooks and folders.
Encourage them to share their notebook and folder policy with their group.

Essential Questions
Ask that teachers determine what the students learned on November 15, and December 2, or any two dates of your choosing. They should go through both notebook piles determining what students learned on the same dates in their classes.

Are there any differences between the two groups: high and low achieving students' notebooks?
Ask them to share any conclusions with their peers.

Ask teachers to examine students' folders from both classes. Request that they make a list of what they find in the folders.

Note: Depending on the culture of the school and/or individual teaching practices, some teachers may be unable to identify what was taught on any given day.
What is the culture of the school as it relates to students' maintaining a notebook and folder for EACH class? What are the challenges?

Distribute the statement and worksheets on the following pages. Discuss

- Ask teachers whether there is a link between keeping a notebook and folder and student achievement-how students perform on quizzes, tests?
- Ask teachers to share or create strategies for ensuring that students bring notebooks and folders to class each day.
- Ask teachers to discuss challenges of implementing a school-wide notebook and folder policy.

I agree/disagree that
A notebook, an ongoing record of what transpires in class, should be the **_equivalent of an ID card in every classroom_** *and thus a requirement for admission. When a student is in the office for a disciplinary problem, the conference should BEGIN with the notebook and folders: "What is your proof that you know why you are here?"*
Without a notebook, or an incomplete notebook, the student is a trespasser in the school and should be treated accordingly.

Teacher Conversations – Working in groups, teachers should agree or disagree with the statement.

Why Students Should Keep a Notebook/Academic Log

Compare this list with the one you created with your group.

1. To open the notebook at the beginning of the period and date it with the day's objective signals readiness to learn.

2. To serve as a way to begin the day's lesson by writing a review of yesterday's lesson.

3. Bell Work should/may be completed in the notebook and collected periodically for assessment. Allocating the first five or ten minutes for this activity helps foster punctuality as well as learning readiness. Bell work should not take half of the instructional period. (See Instructional Time Management for more information.)

4. To serve as a daily account of what goes on in class and to serve as a summary_ of what transpired in class for students who are absent. Instead of asking the teacher what happened, students can ask *several* of their peers to share their notes.

5. To serve as a tool during parent-teacher conferences in order to demonstrate whether or not the student is on task; to further demonstrate what is being covered in class in order to enlist parental support. Request that parents bring the notebook to both scheduled and interim conferences. The notebook serves as a receipt of what the child did or did not learn.

6 To assist with the cohesiveness of the learning process. "Two weeks ago we discussed adaptation (or the elements of a short story, etc.) turn back to that page in your notebook." The date serves as the page number. This strategy keeps the teacher from having to re-teach the entire concept, algorithm, etc. Students can return to that page which serves as a built in review.

7. Writing is a brain-based and brain-friendly activity that supports encoding.

8. Reviewing notes assists with remembering (memory) which is a key foundation of learning and thus preparing for tests and quizzes.

Preparing for Tests, Mid-terms, Final Exams

When a student has difficulty learning a subject, it may not be because s/he is not bright. Often, the student does not know HOW to learn the content. They need to be taught summarizing, paraphrasing, outlining, and note taking techniques in EACH class. Keeping a notebook honors reading and writing in ALL classes.

Too often, the mid-term or final exam becomes whatever the student studied last: the last chapters, the last novel, or the last algorithms. Sometimes this occurs because the culture of the school does support comprehensive mid-term or final exams. It's easier to prepare a test on recently covered material and count it as a double test score grade than it is to go back and select critical concepts from the beginning of the term.

However, students need to be held accountable for ALL information that taught during the term. Learning cannot be solidified without review and the notebook/academic log is the framework that aids in the continuity of learning. Preparing for

Writing is a brain-friendly activity.

comprehensive exams sets the stage for success on state exams which are based on accumulated knowledge. Daily writing is daily practice.

> ➤ **Summarizing Activity**: When students learn to summarize chapters, online information, putting ideas in their own words, they reinforce their knowledge and learn to write concisely.
> ➤ **Paraphrasing** – learning to restate the author's work in their own words and sentence structure. This practice encourages students to finding their own voice with someone else's ideas (textbook or information searched online).
> ➤ **Note taking** from text and the chalkboard/whiteboard supports identifying and separating essential from nonessential information.
> ➤ **Outlining** the chapter for studying for a test supports the hierarchy of information in the text (or information obtained from search engines).

NOTE: These skills will also aid students with their writing assignments, reducing plagiarism, by teaching student how to gather information. 21st century student are fast becoming aggregators of online content (cut and paste) instead of creators of original content.

P.S Students also need to keep a folder for each class with present and past assignments, quizzes, and tests for review.

IV.   **Vocabulary Development**   Research teaches us (Vacca and Vacca) that students need to learn approximately 3000 new words a year to be competitive. We can't teach that many words through rote memorization, but we can teach the vocabulary HABIT. We can demonstrate that there is a pattern to learning words and not all word learning need be by rote memory. A suggestion would be to write three new words daily on the board from the lesson for students to define. The words should be written in a notebook. Each week, repeat five or six of the words with the new ones for reinforcement.

Vocabulary words should show connectedness by theme or structure.

Traditional (no connectedness)	Research-Based
euphoria	omniscient
omnipresent	omnipotent
monotheism	omnivorous
Traditional (no connectedness)	**Research-Based**
euphonious	monotheism
ante meridian	monocular
monocular	monomania

Notebook Assessment: Don't perspire from a paper load of bell work or other notebook activity. The idea is to inspire and not to perspire.

- Give a plus (+) or a minus (–) if the work is complete and/or directions are followed. At the end of the card marking, add up the pluses and minutes and assign a value.
- Give a certain number (five or ten) points **each day** for completion, effort, following directions.
- Inform students that each report cardmarking you will randomly select ten to fifteen dates from the notebook to review and assess.

Note
The idea is to set a standard and not change it. It should become a routine, institutionalized part of the classroom community.

(Student Activity)

Keeping a Notebook/Academic Log

Why We Keep A Notebook (Keep this sheet in your folder)
People who are outstanding in their field generally keep a notebook of some sort: mathematicians, scientists, artists, musicians, athletes (playbook), writers, etc. We will keep a notebook in this class to serve as our personal reservoir or pool of knowledge.

Instructions for Getting Started
1. Maintain a separate spiral notebook for this class. Do not include work from other classes in the notebook.
2. Date and write in the notebook/log **daily**.
3. Write summaries of lectures, concepts; write examples, assignments, board work, bell work. If no work is completed or if class does not meet for any reason, indicate so in the notebook/log. Do NOT tear pages out of your notebook to use as loose-leaf paper. It will cause your spiral to be depleted and you will not be able to take notes. Assignments written on notebook paper will NOT be accepted.
4. Write in the notebooks using a no. 2 pencil or a blue or black ink pen.

The Uses of a Notebook

I   **Bell Work/Do Now**: Problem Solving- We will review work that can completed in five minutes.
Bell Work/Do Now: Complete a diagram, chart, or map. I will give you a graphic of information previously studied to complete: a cell, number chart, a map, story element, etc.

II.   **Timed Writing Activities** - Quick Writes, Impromptu Writes provide practice writing under timed conditions (state exams, ACT) as well as to promote writing fluency.

III   **Summary and Reflections:** Pinpoint where you are having difficulty.
        A The learning process broke down for me when I was reading (identify page, paragraph, section)
        B. The learning process broke down for me when the teacher was explaining…
        C I am still having problems with…

D   A question I would like to ask my teacher is…

E. Today I learned…(write three to five sentences)

F. If you are absent, ask **several** of your peers to share their notes.

Folders:

Maintain a separate folder for this class. In it, you should keep quizzes, tests, and assignments (past and present). Keeping these serve as a receipt of your learning. When it is time for a test, you will be prepared, and there will be NO surprises on report card day.

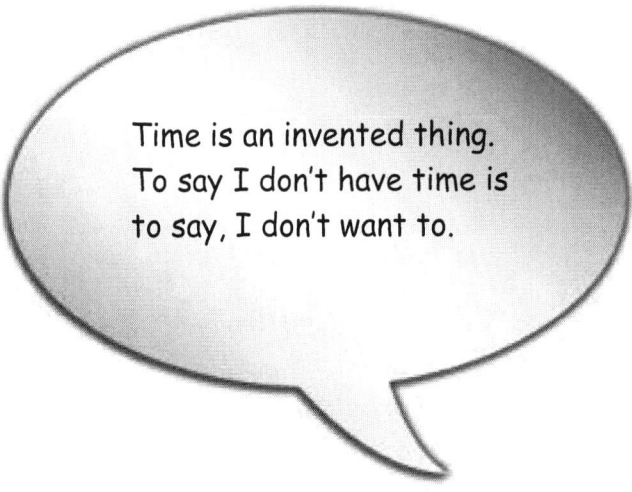

Time is an invented thing. To say I don't have time is to say, I don't want to.

Lao Tzu

No Culture of Notebooks?
No AYP!

(Adequate Yearly Progress)

Creating Systems:
A Clean, Emotionally Safe, and Orderly Community

Guiding Principle 3.6: I have a discipline approach/plan in place that is firm, fair, and consistent. I rarely send students to the office.

Goals: The coach will support teachers as they:
- Create a definition for misbehavior.
- Differentiate between deviant behavior and developmentally normal behavior.
- Identify which behaviors require prevention or intervention strategies on the part of the teacher.
- Identify which behaviors require intervention by the office or an outside support (counselor, parent, psychologist, social worker, etc.)
- Analyze why students are excluded from the classroom.
- Identify the students who are repeatedly sent to the office.
- Investigate behavior patterns in order begin to develop a plan of action.

Materials:
Activities on the next pages
Large Post-it sheets and markers (optional)

Time:
Varies, depending on how many activities you want to complete

Audience:
- Dean of students
- Administrator in charge of discipline
- New teacher coach/mentor
- Leadership teams
- Grade-level teams
- Content area teams

Coaching Support:
Find out which teachers repeatedly send more students to the office than other teachers. Which teachers have exemplary classroom/behavior management? What are their "secrets"? How can you enlist their support? What alliances, building, or district support do you need? Would you like to create a virtual professional learning community around this topic (VPLC)?

Maintenance:
What are the intervention resources provided by the school: counselor? social worker? psychologist?
Distribute the sample behavior management activities and strategies as they are needed (in your judgment) by teachers.

Getting Started

What norms do you need to set? Seating: Think about how you want to arrange the space. Remember the mission and philosophy statement of "an equal voice and an equal regard" when arranging the seating. Community is created when participants can make eye contact with one another.

Parking Lot: You may choose to not answer questions in the middle of delivering a presentation, especially if you are operating under time restraints. Put in place a "question parking lot" where participants can post their questions minimizing interruptions and ensuring all legitimate questions are answered.

Charting/Gallery Walk: Ask groups to chart their responses on a giant Post-it. A great way to share information with the whole group and a great resource for typing up what transpired or was accomplished, it is documentation that can be shared with your virtual professional learning community and/or downloaded as a pdf on the school's website.

NOTE: Before getting started, determine whether or not the school has a uniform discipline plan or approach. What are the strengths and weaknesses of the plan? Has the staff bought into the plan? How can you best support the plan with the teachers?

Background/Conversation

It is up to much debate about the best approach for classroom management. Ultimately it is up to the teacher and the situation to choose what approach will work best to improve student behavior and make the class run as an efficient learning environment. Some leading thinkers on this topic are:

John Dewey: Basic idea was that emphasis should be placed on the broadening of intellect and development through critical thinking of real-world problems, rather than simply on memorization of lessons. This is best accomplished through collaboration.

Abraham Maslow: Believed that human beings' needs are arranged like a ladder. The most basic needs, at the bottom, are physical: air, water, food. Then comes safety needs: security and stability, followed by psychological, or social needs: belonging, love, acceptance. At the top of it all are the self-actualizing needs: the need to fulfill the self, to become all that one is capable of becoming, which is the role of schools to assist. Unfulfilled needs lower on the ladder stop a student from climbing to the next step.

B.F. Skinner: Believed that teachers should supply immediate feedback to students, thus teachers should not allow students to complete additional assignments before giving feedback. This keeps students from continually making the same mistake.

It's easy to conduct an Internet search to find out more about each one, or others, such as **Lee Canter, William Glasser, or Alfie Kohn.**

Added Conversation: What are your insights concerning normal developmental behavior and deviant behavior?

Sample Ice Breaker Questions:

- What is your definition of a discipline problem or misbehavior (See next page)?
- Identify common reasons you send students to the office.
- Have you ever responded to a student's personality rather than to the student's behavior?
- What is your biggest challenge?
- What are your beliefs about student behaviors and teacher responsibility?
- What student behaviors come with the job? In other words, they require prevention and intervention strategies on the part of the **teacher**, not the office.
- What is your discipline policy for your classroom?

CONVERSATIONS
WITH A
COACH

Misbehavior: A Definition

- Interferes with teaching
- Interferes with the rights of others
- Is psychologically/emotionally unsafe
- Is physically unsafe
- Destroys property of others

Patterns of Misbehavior

Goal: to identify the patterns in the classroom, as well as to identify the students who exhibit the behaviors. Which are NORMAL DEVELOPMENTAL (they come with the job), and which are DEVIANT (require outside intervention)?

Typical Behavior Patterns	Which ones predominate in the classroom?	Primary Student Violators
1. **Verbal Interruptions:** talking, humming, laughing, calling out, whispering.		
2. **Off Task** –Inattentive: daydreaming, sleeping, combing hair, playing with something, doodling.		
3. **Movement:** passing notes, sitting on top of desk, sitting two legs of a chair, throwing paper/airplanes		
4. **Disrespect –** Student to teacher or student to student: arguing, profanity, vulgarity		

Patterns of Misbehavior, continued

Typical Behavior Patterns	Which ones predominate in the classroom?	Primary Student Violators
5. Violence/Fighting		
6. Bullying (Is there a school policy in place?)		
7. Extortion/Coercion		
8. Chronic Insubordination		
9. Destruction of Property		
10. Cell Phone/Electronic Devices		
11. Other		

Patterns of Misbehavior

1.

Which behaviors are normal development behaviors and which are deviant behaviors? Why?

2.   Which are the top five behaviors that predominate in your classroom?

3.   Which three to five students are repeatedly sent to the office and for what behaviors?

4.   Who <u>owns</u> the behavior problem(s) and why? (students? teachers? society? community? parents?)

5.   Is your classroom a hostile learning environment? If so, which behaviors cause it to be so? What can you do about it? What support do you need?

Classroom Community Goals: (Student Activity)

Goals:
- ✓ To develop a community in which troublesome behavior is solved together.
- ✓ To reflect on how we can live and learn together.

Activity: At the beginning of each card marking, we will discuss, establish, revise, and/or reinforce goals/rules and needs for the classroom community.

After studying the Behavior Pattern Chart, we will develop a plan.

What Classroom Rules Do We Need?	Why?

Rules will be broken. How they are handled will make or break OUR classroom community.

Student Activity

A Character Education Approach to Behavior

When students misbehave, they are really stealing time from themselves and their classmates, which is quite unfair.

Because of your behavior, you are being temporarily excluded from class. You must complete this form and have it signed by a parent before you can return to class.

A.   Why have you been referred to the office or are being excluded from class?

B.   What is your outstanding trait or talent? Explain.

C.   How does your behavior need to improve so that you are an asset to the classroom?

D.   What are your academic goals?

E.   What are your work/career goals?

F. Describe your attendance.

G. Do you owe your classmates an apology?

H Doctors write prescriptions for patients in order for them to get well. Write out an analysis/explanation of your behavior and a prescription for changing it.

Your Signature   Date

Parent's Signature   Date

Phone and e-mail address

My Story, My Side

Name   Grade
Homeroom teacher   Birth date

      Every story has two sides. What is your side? Begin by identifying the **key elements** and then write your story. Remember to use your best capitalization, spelling, and grammar. Your story represents you.

1.   What is today's date and time?

2.   What was the time and place of the incident?

3   What are the names of the people involved? Tell something about them.

4.   What is/was the PROBLEM/CONFLICT?

5.   What is the resolution? How did it end?

What LESSON(S) have you learned about (gossip, respect, honesty, fear, responsibility, anger, loyalty, friendship, violence, choices, courage, etc.)?

My Story, My Side

Now that you have identified the key elements of your story, write your story in your best "VOICE" AND your best PENMANSHIP.

It all started...

Your Signature   Date

Teachable Moments
The Teacher as Preacher, Flatterer, Aphorist, Booster, Parent

Rationale: Discipline provides a moral code that makes it possible for the small society of a classroom to function. The classroom is a social system that is predicated on the need to impart morals and values, as well as skills/knowledge. Through quotes, quips, and aphorisms, we help learners to discover the things within themselves they had not suspected were there. Students need a nurturing environment in order to be able to nurture when their turn as adults come. Discipline without moral/character education is merely "crowd control" (Thomas Lickona, Educating *for Character*).

In the place of a sarcastic or caustic remark, an appropriate quote sometimes instructs with both a sting and wisdom.

"Winners never quit; quitters never win."
—Unknown

"Nothing is really work unless you would rather be doing something else."
—Barrie

"He that is good for making excuses is seldom good for anything else."
—Franklin

"Sin has many tools, but a lie is the handle which fits them all."
—Holmes

"Since we cannot get what we like, let us like what we can get."
—Spanish proverb

"It is hard to fail, but it is worse never to have tried to succeed."
—Theodore Roosevelt

"Thinking is the hardest work there is, which is the probable reason so few engage in it."
—Henry Ford

"It is much easier to be critical than to be correct."
—Disraeli

"The truth is always the strongest argument."
—Sophocles

"The way to be nothing is to do nothing."
—Howe

"The manner of speaking is as important as the matter."
—Chesterfield

"Light is the task where many share the toil."
—Homer

"A (wo)man must take the fat with the lean."
—Dickens

"Not to know is bad; not to wish to know is worse."
—African proverb

"We are what we repeatedly do; excellence then is not an act, but a habit."
—Aristotle

"Treat people as if they were what they ought to be, and you help them become what they are capable of being."
—Goethe

"Education is our passport to the future, for tomorrow belongs to the people who prepare for it today."
—Malcolm X

"When we build fences to keep others out, we erect barriers to keep others down. We keep ourselves in and hold ourselves down; and the barriers we erect against others become prison bars to our souls."

—Dr. Benjamin Mays

"It is not a disaster to be unable to capture your ideal, but it is a disaster to have no ideal to capture. It is not a disgrace not to reach the stars, but it is a disgrace to have no stars to reach for—not failure, but low aim is a sin."
—Dr. Benjamin Mays

"A person without a goal will self-destruct."

—Dr. Benjamin Mays

"Education is not only about becoming smart; it is also about developing character."
—Albert Shanker

"All life must be worked at—protected, planted, replanted, fashioned, cooked for, coaxed, diapered, formed, sustained. Work is the way that we tend to the world."

—Lance Morrow

Add your own quotes or sayings.

The more there will be laws, the more there will be thieves.

Lao Tzu

Owl Mountain Coaching Forms and Templates

Appendix A

These forms are a starting point and will keep you from having to make up everything as you go. These instruments provide a convenient and consistent approach for those working as part of a team or a cadre of coaches. Feel free to revise them as you situation dictates.

Nomination/Support Form

In order to increase teacher and departmental efficacy, identify teachers or groups that would **benefit** from coaching or additional support. Also, identify teachers with assets who can support others.

Teacher's Name	Grade Level	Room Location	Department	Assets
			English Language Arts	
			English Language Arts	
			English Language Arts	
			Science	
			Science	
			Science	
			Social Studies	
			Social Studies	
			Social Studies	
			Math	
			Math	
			Math	
			Other (grade level, content level)	
			Other (grade level, content level)	
			Other	

Administrative Approval_____ Date_____

Getting to Know You

Demographics/Rapport-Building/Demonstrating Care

Coaching Goal: To develop a pool of knowledge about individual teachers you support.

Note: It will take several "chats" to glean this information from teachers. It is well worth the time investment. Remember Mother Teresa: I don't care how much you know until I know how much you care.

Name of teacher   **Content area**

1. Age Range of Teacher

2. Experience in Other Schools

3. Certification—Lack of Certification—Alternative Certification—Second Career-Teach for America

4. Advanced Degrees (Masters and Beyond)

5. Average Years of Service

Life issues/challenges: What is going on inside of the teacher's head and heart (marriage, divorce, family, children, health, other)?

Hobbies, interests:

Owl Mountain Coaching Unique Teaching Profile

Identifying the Assets: Abilities, Beliefs, Skills, Strengths

Teacher's Name _____ Grade Level_____

Department/Content Area _____

What are the unique abilities, beliefs, and talents as they relate to one of the core areas? Write a statement on how you can assist teachers to build alliances and develop relationships with peers by sharing their gifts. Complete three forms for each teacher.

1.0 Establishing Credibility	**2.0 Demonstrating Care**
3.0 Creating Systems: Rituals and Routines	

Abilities, Beliefs, Skills, Strengths that can be leveraged to share with others and thus increase school assets: Identify the principles.

Growth Needed: Undeveloped or underdeveloped—Identify the principles:

Commitment/Relationships needed to share or build assets:

Gaining Entry: Reinforcing Credibility

Create a brochure or form of your own design. Study the one on the next page; it is unique to my strengths as a literacy coach. Think about the additional services you can provide. Because you are not an administrator, you must be strategic about encouraging others to pay attention to you and to the issues that you want to raise. The form is one protocol for establishing and or reinforcing your credibility. In effect, you are saying, "This is what I have to offer." If you fail to establish credibility, you will find teachers resistant to accepting your support. Often, they will wonder how you came to be a coach in the first place and may not allow you to enter their classrooms. This is especially true for veteran teachers, who may see you as someone without a classroom and, therefore, without responsibility.

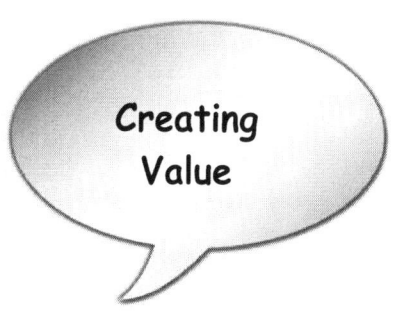
Creating Value

Suggestion: Distribute the form personally to EACH teacher and take a few minutes to chat about something **_personal_** to ensure that relationships are developed. A week or so later, place another copy in mailboxes (with the permission of the administration). Follow up by visiting the teachers again, individually, to determine if they have completed the form. If not, provide them with another form.

If teachers are reluctant to ask for assistance, ask to be assigned to new or marginal teachers. See the nomination form in this appendix.

Coaching Support: As you begin to gain entry, think about how you will share what's going on in teachers' classrooms without betraying the confidentially necessary for your coaching relationship. This is a good opportunity to think about how to empower teachers to form alliances and to request peer support. You may want to meet with your learning community.

Dear _____,

My name is _____ and I am the coach assigned to your school.
I am available for direct assistance INSIDE and OUTSIDE the classroom in one or more of the following areas:

Select	Support Areas	Comment
1.	**Establishing Credibility** Teaching voice Body language Other	
2.	**Demonstrating Care** Bonding and connecting activities Bulletin boards Seating plan Collaborative learning/Synergy groups Other	
3.	**Creating Systems** Syllabus Time management Notebook and folder system Assessment/grading/rubrics Classroom discipline/behavior management Other	
4.	Lesson Planning	
5.	Reading Across the Curriculum Strategies	
6.	Writing Across the Curriculum Strategies/Peer response groups	
7.	Systematic Vocabulary Development	
8. .	Project-Based Learning	
9.	Using Technology to ENHANCE Learning (TV, Movies, Web Quests, Social Networks, Search Engine Research, etc.	
10.	Literature/Research Articles	
11.	Other	

Educator's Name   Location

Owl Mountain Coaching Formative and Summative Assessment Tools

Appendix B

"Not everything that can be counted counts and not everything that counts can be counted."
—Sign on the wall in
Albert Einstein's office

Crafting a Scope of Service and Teacher Quality Plan

You may choose to share the items below with your professional learning community or to reflect on them in your journal.

The three scope of service charts on the next pages will help as you craft a plan of action, a plan that impacts teacher quality, classroom practices, and reduces attrition. They can also be use as formative and summative assessment tools.
As you review the charts, think about:

- What are the teaching quality and classroom practice assets of the school? Where are the gaps: undeveloped or underdeveloped?

- What _joint accountabilities_ do you need to establish with the leadership team/administrators? What "conversations" do you want to hold with them?

- What are the priorities and timelines? Do you need to create a calendar?

- How will you motivate teachers to build alliances and support one another: a shared sense of responsibility?

- Will you encourage teachers to keep their own journals or to create a professional learning community of their own?

- What differences will you encounter when coaching a new teacher, an unsatisfactory teacher, and/or a veteran teacher? How will you approach each?

1.0   Establishing Credibility Scope of Service –Agenda Building, Formative, and Summative Assessment.

What Are the Intangible Forces, Beliefs, Attitudes?	
1.1	Teachers create stability as well as credibility because their attendance is better than the district average.	*School Culture*
1.2	Teachers dress for success. Each day they dress as if they are going to the workplace.	*School Culture*
1.3	Most teachers' voices are clear and confident rather than weak and barely audible.	
1.4	Most teachers' nonverbal body language demonstrates a positive, confident bearing rather than one that is unsure or easily intimidated.	
1.5	Most teachers' *general temperament* exhibits patience and understanding rather than anger and frustration.	
1.6	Most teachers exhibit "WITHITNESS". They are aware of classroom surroundings, happenings, and students' actions at ALL times.	

2.0   Demonstrate Caring Scope of Service - Agenda Building, Formative and Summative Assessment

	What Are the Intangible Forces, Beliefs, Attitudes?	
2.1	The teachers know and can call ALL of *their* students by name.	*School Culture*
2.2	Teachers are aware that community is people with whom we share our stories, promoting a sense of belonging. Students engage in "Bonding" or "Getting to Know You Activities."	
2.3	The teachers circulate to assist and to insist that students work rather than constantly sit their desks. A "We" are in this together attitude prevails.	*School Culture*
2.4	The teachers create bulletin boards that display students' work and promote a caring but rigorous learning environment.	*School Culture*
2.5	The teachers are aware of the interpersonal dynamics in my classroom. They have seating plans in place that create stability and community.	*School Culture*
2.6	The teachers are aware of the interconnectedness of humans and promote a classroom community where students work collaboratively as well as independently: Interdependence and Individual Accountability.	The teacher IS/IS NOT the "sage on stage."

3.0 Creating Systems Scope of Service - Agenda Building, formative and summative assessment tools.

	What Are the Intangible Forces, Beliefs, Attitudes?	
3.1	Teachers have developed a syllabus that outlines the framework for success from August/September through June/July.	*School Culture*
3.2	Teachers have rituals/routines in place that make good use of time at the beginning of the period, the end (closure) of the period and preclude lost of instructional time.	
3.3	Teachers require and MONITOR that students bring a notebook and folder to class EACH day because they aid memory and the continuity of the learning process.	*School Culture*
3.4	Teachers give **comprehensive** midterm assessments and comprehensive final assessments because learning is cumulative (state-mandated tests are based on comprehensive knowledge and skills).	*School Culture*
3.5	Teachers' system for assessment (grading) is rarely challenged by students, parents, or the office because it is public, consistent, and ongoing. Students understand their strength/improvement areas and can compute their grades on their own.	*The teacher IS/IS NOT the "sole" arbiter of excellence.*
3.6	Teachers have a discipline approach/plan in place that is firm, fair, and consistent. They seldom send students to the office.	

Barriers to Transformation/Change

Stuck in the *Status* Quo

Apathy

Power of the Familiar

Entrenched Habits and Practices

Teacher Temperament

Teacher as the Sole Arbiter of Excellence

Belief Systems

"Sage on Stage"

"Soliloquizing Authority"

Inertia

"Running with the Gazelles, Eating with the Lions"
African Proverb

Every morning in Africa, a gazelle wakes up.
It knows that it must run faster than the fastest lion or it will be killed.

Every morning a lion wakes up.
It knows it must outrun the slowest gazelle or it will starve to death.

It doesn't matter whether you are a lion or a gazelle.
When the sun comes up, you had better start running.

In a global economy, we are ALL temps!

Assessing Teacher Assets Writing Assignment

Goal: Coaches will support teachers as they:
Identify their **assets**, developed, underdeveloped, undeveloped.
Explore the value they bring to the classroom and to the school.
Create an e-mail to convince the administration they should be rehired.

Materials Needed:
African proverb and transformation chart on the previous pages.
Script/conversation below; writing activity on next page.

Time Needed:
The writing assignment requires 30 minutes—ACT format.

Who is the audience for this activity?

- ✓ Content or grade-level meetings
- ✓ One-on-one teacher support
- ✓ Professional Development Days (Whole faculty)
- ✓ Selected group of teachers

Coaching Support:
What relationships or alliances do you need to build in order to make this activity successful? Highly effective teachers? Leadership team? Virtual Professional Learning Community. **I would recommend the leadership team/principal.**

Maintenance:
Because this is a formative assessment activity, what follow-up is necessary?

Instructions:
Encourage participants to sit in a formation that honors all voices.
Review the three core areas for building a classroom community. Ask participants to share within their groups.

This activity makes a good beginning and end of the school year (pre and post assessment) activity.

Background/Conversation

Share the proverb and list of the barriers to change/reform (previous pages), as well as the information written below before completing the writing assignment.

Historically, teachers' salaries have been negotiated as a unit, with everyone placed on a salary schedule based on the amount of education and the years of experience. Educators with effective classroom management skills, positive parental and peer relationships, and a low failure rate generally have enjoyed the stability and security of a lifetime teaching contract. No more!

Enter the innovative forces of technology, along with the unruly forces of globalization and presto, a new set of teacher expectations enter the schoolhouse. These forces necessitate a task educators have never been REQUIRED or NEEDED to do before—teach problem-seeking and problem-solving to the masses. And to the children who come to us with wounded souls and who must suddenly measure up no matter what specific deficits they bring. We can no longer use socioeconomic factors as an excuse for poor achievement, for failing to teach under adverse conditions.

Increasingly, school boards and school districts hold schools accountable for improved test scores within a clean, safe, and orderly environment. Increasingly, principals control their own budgets, and control hirings and firings. Parents who are unhappy vote with their feet and take their children, along with their per-pupil allotment worth thousands of dollars, to another school or district. Translated: Unsuccessful schools are restructured and principals' contracts are not renewed. Tenure and defined pensions are gone with the wind.

Added Conversations: Add your experience and expertise.

Ask Teachers:

- How do they now establish credibility with students. What is their brand? What do they stand for?
- How do they now demonstrate caring (building a rigorous community with a heart)?
- What new systems have they now created?

CONVERSATIONS
WITH A
COACH

Brand Teacher Writing Prompt

The prompts listed below are written in the ACT writing format. ACT time allocation is thirty minutes.

The Last Monopoly

I.   Fired or Rehired   (30 Minutes)

All educators are now on an annual contract. Administrators determine whether or not teachers should be retained or released at the end of the school year. Under the new system, salary is also negotiated at the end of the year. It is NOT automatic. Prepare an e-mail that will **persuade** your administrator to renew your contract and/or to give you a salary increase. You may use the Owl Mountain Coaching™ Asset-Mapping principles as part of your strategy. What **opposition** might you anticipate from your administrator? How will you **respond** to her opposition?

THINK: What are your strengths (assets)?

How will the administrator **reply**? Do you have any "liabilities" (underdeveloped or undeveloped assets)?

What is your **response** to the **opposition**/administrator?

Fired or Rehired Assessment Guidelines

- ❏ Thesis statement (umbrella statement)
- ❏ Unity (sticks to the topic)
- ❏ Insight
- ❏ Persuasive and anticipates an opposing viewpoint (coherence, organization)
- ❏ Language choices
- ❏ Syntax—sentence structure
- ❏ Grammar and mechanics

Coaches are dedicated to providing ongoing opportunities to engage teachers in reflective, but sometimes *critical* conversations about teaching quality and classroom practices.

Owl Mountain Coaching
Personal Challenge Four

Journal Entry: You're Fired

"Writing holds us responsible for our words and ultimately make us more thoughtful human beings." Ernest Boyer

Dear Coach,

You have been working for up to one year with at least one teacher who cannot or will not improve. Teaching does not seem to suit her. Prepare a "conversation" to **persuade (**the teacher AND/OR the school's administration) that **perhaps** he/she is not right for this position. Articulate your concerns*: succinctly, clearly,* AND *diplomatically*. You may use the Owl Mountain Coaching Asset-Mapping Principles™ as part of your strategy. What **opposition** might you anticipate from the teacher/administration? How will you **respond to** any arguments?

Feedback - emotionally neutral information
Criticism - emotional and subjective; triggers defensive response; causes confrontation;

Remember, you are not a supervisor, but a peer.

Sincerely,

Lorraine Richardson, Chief Owl

Notes

"We don't receive wisdom; we must discover it for ourselves after a journey that no one can take for us or spare us." Marcel Proust

Darwin Rules:
Be Distinct or Be Extinct!
Make History or Be History!

Reflecting on the Journey: Self-Assessment

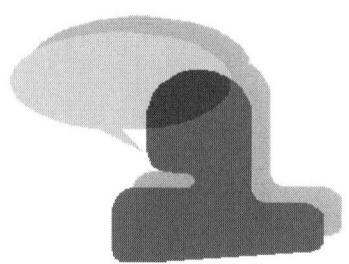

It's been a year since started on "your journey" of supporting teachers as they journeyed from working in classrooms based on a factory model of compliance to a twenty-first century classroom model based on community. How have you fared? Respond to the list below in your journal and/or with your professional learning network.

Reflection is the magic dust of improvement.
John Dewey

The Mission: As coaches, we are committed to stemming the tide of teacher attrition that is critical to student achievement.

i. Formative/Summative Mapping—End of the first term or a selected target point

Identify the assets/principles where teachers are improving or have improved.

What assets still remain undeveloped or underdeveloped? Why?
What factors/traits cause some teachers to improve their practice while others stagnate?

II. Describe how successful YOU have been as a coach:

1. Establishing Credibility with staff?
2. Demonstrating Care?
3. Creating Systems (rituals and routines)?

III. What alliances have been built to mobilize and sustain the teaching talent relationships needed to improve student achievement?

IV.   What can/will teachers verbalize about your efforts to support their teaching practices?

V.   What are your successes or wins as a coach, and can others REPLICATE them?

VI.   What were your frustrations/obstacles as a coach? What did you do about them?

VII.   What issues have you faced as a coach/teacher leader trying to make changes without formal authority?

VIII.   What advice would you provide to a teacher who wants to be a coach?

IX.   **Metrics:**   *What was the scope of your impact as a coach?*

    A.   Fewer classroom discipline referrals?
    B.   Lower classroom/student failures?
    C.   Improved student attendance?
    D.   Improved assessment/grading practices?
    E.   Fewer parental complaints?
    F.   Improved teacher attendance?
    G.   Other: Explain!

Challenge: What personal lessons have you learned about teacher attrition in your school or district?

Dear Trusted Professional,

Within *A Coach's Guide to Asset-Mapping Teacher Quality: The Journey from Compliance to Community,* you have uncovered concrete principles for why some teachers enjoy enormous success with students without seeming to try, while others struggle or fail. Hopefully, you have been able to spearhead replicating and spreading throughout the school, content, or grade levels the beliefs, skills, and capacities (the assets) these naturals take for granted. Often, it is not a lack of teachers' content knowledge or intellectual firepower that causes failure, but their inability to shape a high-performance learning community that empowers ALL students to maximize their potential. As you have modified and built on the Owl Mountain Coaching Asset-Mapping System™, you have distilled your own success secrets for working with teachers.

Be the Change!

Optimistically, I hope this workbook also laid a framework for you to create or join a virtual professional learning community (VPLC) that taps into the insights and amplifies the thought processes of coaches in other locations throughout America and indeed the globe. It is no longer necessary to go it alone. However, more than ever, American education is under siege, brought on by the forces of technology and globalization. Schools and especially teachers are bearing the brunt of an implacable anger. As you navigate an uncertain environment, you won't get by unscathed, either, as you will need to justify your existence every day. Expect to engage in hard "conversations" about the beliefs, skills, and capacities you possess (your assets) that qualify you to instruct and support others.

As you juggle an intimidating number of priorities, your key function and role is to hold in memory the *unique teaching profile/* (assets, developed and underdeveloped) for EACH teacher. You are the keeper and communicator of the vision for the teaching quality and classroom practices necessary to build a twenty-first century learning community for ALL of our children to succeed.

Mahatma Gandhi said, "Be the change you want to see in the world." I say that you are the change; you are the reform/transformation that we need to see in our schools.

Owl Mountain Coaching Final Challenge

Journal Entry: I Am the Change!

"Writing holds us responsible for our words and ultimately makes us more thoughtful human beings." Ernest Boyer

Dear Coach,

The unruly forces of globalization and technological change have moved to disrupt an educational system created during the era of industrialization, during a social and economic context that did not expect to or need to educate ALL children equally and well.

The same forces are shifting educators from a world of tenure and stability to a world of performance like in profit-making fields. Whether we like it or not, the roles of schools and all educators are being re-conceptualized, reinvented, and re-imagined.

You were hired to improve teacher quality and ultimately reduce teacher attrition in order to advance student achievement. Did you?

Prepare a final "conversation" with the leadership team/school administers/client to convince them that a line item for your services should be included in next year's budget. Why should you be rehired, your contract renewed? Do you deserve a bonus?

What **value** did you bring to the table? How do you measure or assess your impact? What are your **assets**?

What **opposition** do you expect from the client? What were your liabilities? How will you respond? What will you do differently next time?

Sincerely,

Lorraine Richardson, Chief Owl

Notes

"We don't receive wisdom; we must discover it for ourselves after a journey that no one can take for us or spare us." Marcel Proust

Afterword

Implementation—A Tale of Three Visionaries

I attended a Harvard Graduate School of Education's week-long Project Zero Summer Institute. During a closing session, the powers-that-be shared with us that often innovations, programs, or reforms aren't successful because they lack three needed visionaries for change: a conceptual visionary, a power visionary, and a day-to-day visionary. They are not, generally, embodied in one person.

Conceptual Visionary: As the coach, teacher leader, or other trusted professional, you are the reform. A Coach's Guide to *Asset-Mapping Teacher Quality: The Journey from Compliance to Community* is a conceptual guide, a vision based on my fifteen plus years of instructional and literacy coaching that you can build upon, integrating your own expertise, experience, and wisdom.

Power Visionary: As the power visionary, the principal or school leader must send a message to staff by providing the necessary resources, allocating the time, and demonstrating the courage that this is the change/reform needed. In some circles, the power visionary is also called an SOB. **Motto**: We can; we will; we must!

Day-to-Day Visionary: Who is minding the store? So much slips through the cracks in schools because we wear so many hats, juggle so many responsibilities. However, at *least one* onsite educator/administrator MUST hold in memory the **unique teaching profile** (asset map) for each teacher, EACH DAY. Managing by spending thirty minutes or more **daily** in and out of classroom, this visionary sends the message: *"I care; I'm concerned; I'm curious."* A message is also sent to students that a leader has the teacher's back. What are each teacher's strengths? What areas are undeveloped or underdeveloped? Where are teachers on the continuum? What alliances are being or have been built to mobilize and sustain the human/teaching capital relationships needed for change? In a large school, the day-to-day visionary's task may be managed by several content or grade-level leaders.

Schools are in the CIA **business**: *Curriculum, Instruction, and Assessment*. The classroom community is the FOUNDATION upon which teaching and learning are built. And teachers are a school's greatest human capital for closing the achievement gap.

Sincerely,

Lorraine Richardson, Chief Owl

Bibliography

Costa, Arthur and Garmston, Robert *Cognitive Coaching*, Michigan: Christopher Gordon Publishing,1994.

Danielson, Charlotte, *Enhancing Professional Practice: A Framework for Teaching*, Virginia, Assoc. Supervision and Curriculum Development,1996.

Friedman, Thomas, *The World Is Flat*, New York: Farrar, Straus, Giroux, 2005

Friere, Paulo, *The Pedagogy of the Oppressed*, New York: Continuum Press,1994.

Gardner, Howard, Csikzentmihalyl, Mihaly Damon, William Good, *Work: When Ethics and Excellence Meet*, New York: Basic Books, 2001

Gerber, Michael, *The E-Myth Revisited*, New York: HarperCollins, 2000

Glickman, Carl D., *Leadership for Learning: How to Help Teachers Succeed*, Virginia: Assoc. Supervision and Curriculum Development, 2002

Hayashi, Shawn Kent, *Conversations for Change*, New York: McGraw Hill, 2011.

Hill, Napoleon, *Think and Grow Rich, New York: Soho Books, 1938*

Himmele, Persida and Himmele, William, *Total Participation Techniques*, Virginia: ASCD, 2011.

Hunter, Madeline, *Mastery Teaching*, University of California, Los Angeles: Tip Publication, 1982

Kretzmann, John P. and McKnight, John L., *Building Communities from the Inside Out: A Path toward Finding and Mobilizing a Community's Assets*, Evanston, Ill. Center for Urban Affair and Policy Research Neighborhood Innovations Network, Northwestern University, 1993

Kohn, Alfie, *Beyond Discipline: From Compliance to Community*, Virginia: Assoc. for Supervision and Curriculum Development, 1996

LaBarre, Polly and Taylor, Bill Mavericks, *At Work: Why the Most Original Minds in Business Win*, Harper Collins, New York, 2006

Lassonde, Cynthia A. and Israel, Susan E., *Teacher Collaboration for Professional Learning; Facilitating Study, Research, and Inquiry Communities,*

Jossey-Bass, San Francisco, 2010

Levin, James and James Nolan, *Principles of Classroom Management*, Massachusetts: Allyn and Bacon, 1991

Lickona, Thomas, *Educating for Character: How Our Schools Can Teach Respect and Responsibility*, New York: Bantam Books, 1991

Martz, Larry, *Making Schools Better*, New York: Times Books, 1992

Marzano, Robert J., *Transforming Classroom Grading*, Virginia: Assoc. for Supervision and Curriculum Development, 2000

Seymour, Daniel and Terry Seymour, *America's Best Classrooms*, Princeton, New Jersey: Peterson's Guides, 1992

Strong, Peter, *Community: The Structure of Belonging*, San Francisco, Berrett-Koehler, 2008

Suarez-Orazco Marcelo and Desiree Baolian Qin-Hilliard, *Globalization: Culture and Education in the New Millennium*, Berkeley, Los Angeles: University of California Press, 2004

Tapscott, Don and Williams, Anthony D., *Wikinomics: How Mass Collaboration Changes Everything*, Penguin Group, New York, 2006

Toffler, Alvin, *Future Shock*, Random House, New York, 1970

Toffler, Alvin, *The Third Wave*, Bantam Books, New York, 1980

Wolfe, Patricia, *Brain Matters: Translating Research into Classroom Practice*, Virginia: Assoc. for Supervision and Curriculum Development, 2001

Selected Internet Links

These links were active at the time this document was completed, but may have become unconnected due to changes beyond my control.

ASCD Learn Teach Lead; www.ascd.org

Asset-Based Community Development Institute: http://www.abcdinstitute.org/

Brickman, Chuck, Maslow's Theory of Hierarchical Needs—Alive and Well in the Classroom: http://teachers.net/gazette/JAN03/brickman.html

Compton, Robert: www.2mminutes.com. Regardless of nationality, as soon as a student completes the eighth grade, the clock starts on the two million minutes they have until they complete high school.

Coaches in the High School Classroom: Studies in Implementing High School Reform. The forty-four-page publication, *Coaches in the High School Classroom*, features close-ups of six coaches in Boston and Houston. Intended to provide fuel for discussion, the portraits are interspersed with guiding questions and followed by several tools that can be used for further discussion, assessment, and analysis of coaching programs (2005): http://www.annenberginstitute.org/resources/tl.html

Developing A Discipline Plan for You by Thomas H. Allen, Ph.D.: http://www.humboldt.edu/~tha1/discip-options.html

Flowers, Joe, Interview of Ronald Heifetz: Leadership without Easy Answers: www.well.com/~bbear/heifetz.html.

Heifetz, Robert, The nature of adaptive leadership: www.youtube.com/watch?v=QfLLDvn0pI8
Leadership without Easy Answers, interview of Harvard University leadership expert Ronald Heifetz, by Joe Flowers.

Knight, Jim: http://www.instructionalcoach.org/ (Kansas Coaching Project)

Mass Insight's 2007 Gates-funded report **The Turnaround Challenge:** www.massinsight.org/turnaround/reports.aspx

McMillan, Michael, *Big Ideas in Little Books* online course: http://www.ed2go.com

Neufeld, Barbara and Dana Roper, "Coaching: A Strategy for Developing Instructional Capacity" (the paper describes what coaching is, what coaches do, the kinds of supports that coaches need, and the potential benefits to both educators and students; the forty-eight-page paper is available in print and as a pdf document): http://www.annenberginstitute.org/resources/tl.html

No Child Left Behind: http://www.ed.gov

Obama-Biden Education Plan www.change.org

Putnam, Robert: http://www.bowlingalone.com/ (website for *Bowling Alone: The Collapse and Revival of American Community*)

Zimmerman, Mark: Emotional Literacy Language and Vocabulary—How to Make the World a Better Place:
http://emotionalliteracyeducation.com/emotional-literacy-language-vocabulary.shtml

Lorraine Richardson
Instructional and Literacy Coach/Consultant/Trainer
Owl Mountain Coaching Asset-Mapping System™ Creator

"Chief Owl"

Lorraine is a skilled, urban educator who taught at both the middle and high school levels, gaining a tremendous insight into the anatomy of a high-performing classroom community. For over fifteen years, she served the Detroit Metropolitan Area as a literacy coach and as an instructional specialist, coaching teachers in the classroom and designing professional development activities. She has created and authored hundreds of documents to improve teacher quality and classroom practices. As a former co-director of the National Writing Project: Metro-Detroit, she trained hundreds of teachers in the writing process. She has also served as a consultant for Michigan Virtual School, an online learning provider.

Lorraine earned a Master's Degree in Public Administration from Wayne State University in Detroit, Michigan and a Bachelor of Science Degree in Education from Ohio University in Athens, Ohio

To expand her professional horizons, Lorraine attended Harvard University's Project Zero and also enrolled in their online learning course, Teaching to Standards Using New Technologies. The study of Curriculum Construction and Supervision of Instruction has further enhanced her instructional knowledge.

She is Chief Visionary Officer at Conversations with a Coach and "Chief Owl" at Owl Mountain Coaching. Lorraine can be reached at:

lrichardson@conversationswithacoach.com
http://www.owlmountaincoaching.com
www.twitter.com/lyrichardson
313 690-9364

—

Owl Mountain Coaching Presents:

Seminars, Speaking Engagements, Parent Meetings, Virtual Professional Learning Community Support (VPLC).

I.   Revise This Guide   Customize the coaching guide to suit your situation/school/or district. Integrate your storehouse of experience, expertise, insights, and wisdom into the Owl Mountain Coaching System™ and into the "conversations."

II.   1+1 = 3   Using Social Media to Unleash the Synergy/Energy of Coaches: Why Mass Collaboration Works! Through virtual collaboration, communication, and cooperation coaching teams become a virtual senate of connected and committed educators working to construct a new and collective knowledge about teacher quality and coaching practices in their institution. (School Districts-Teams)

III.   Assessment: What Do Grades Have to Do with It? True assessment should be a two-way process that is carried out through interaction between the teacher and the learner. Students should know and understand their current level of performance. When they don't, their grades become a source of conflict, and the learning community breaks down as grades are challenged by students, parents, and/or administrators. Coaches/Parents will learn to work with teachers to develop a system that is clear, transparent, and ongoing.

IV.   Classroom Management: Data and Patterns Rules will be broken, how they are handled will make or break the classroom community. In this interactive seminar, coaches/parents will learn to audit classroom behaviors, engage in data-driven "Conversations", and examine belief systems about student behavior and teacher/parent responsibility.

V.   Collaborative Learning: Promoting Social and Intellectual Exchange
Collaborative learning is the infrastructure that is designed to support authentic learning. It is the foundation for shared reading, project-based learning, argumentation and debate,, critical thinking, and the writing process.

VI.   **Speech Topics**:   Teacher Equity and the Attrition Challenge
Teacher 2.0 and Classroom Transformation

VII.   Ask about our Writing and/or Reading Across the Curriculum Series.

Printed in Great Britain
by Amazon